TABLE OF CONTENTS

GOD'S WISDOM FOR TODAY'S CHALLENGES

BIBLE STORIES
for Teens

EXPLORE YOUR FAITH, OVERCOME OBSTACLES
BUILD UNSHAKEABLE RESILIENCE
AND DISCOVER LIFE'S PURPOSE

RADIANT FAITH

INTRODUCTION

In the beginning . . . There has to be a beginning, and you have found it. Believer or non-believer, because you live in a culture that has Judeo-Christian roots, you have likely been exposed to stories found in the Bible whether you realized it or not. You may think that you already know the stories that are presented in this paraphrased version, but my guess is that as you read this book, you will find that most of the stories are much deeper than you realize and that they may apply to your life in ways that you have never considered. As you would expect, there is an application for religious growth; however, most of the stories remain popular in culture because there is also an application for the secular person as well.

The following are fifty of the most familiar Bible stories, twenty-five from the Old Testament and twenty-five from the New Testament. Each story is titled as it is known in pop culture and then retold in contemporary English, making it a joy to read as it was intended to be. The story is followed by a brief devotional examining a life lesson that the story teaches, followed by questions to help one apply the lesson to daily life. If you are intrigued to read the original version, scripture references are provided. Each story concludes with an affirmation, a brief, easy-to-memorize gem that sums up the story's lesson.

The Bible may have been written long ago, but its teachings still have relevance today. The Bible is full of life lessons, and many of these teachings are especially relevant to youth. From "overcoming giants" to "breaking down walls," we're being asked to do it all. These stories provide insight into tough questions, such as: what is the secret to contentment? Is it okay to tell white lies? Why do bad things happen to good people? And is it okay to have questions about religion? Also, as teens, we are trying to come up with our own system of values and ethics we can truly believe in rather than parroting our parents and friends, and these stories challenge us to think through a wide variety of issues.

The stories can be read in any order; they can all stand alone. To understand the flow of the Bible's story, though, they did need to be read in order. However, should you be asked to present a devotional at camp, you can choose any story, and everyone will be able to enjoy it. You can also share your favorite stories with your siblings, reading them to sleep at night. In fact, there are numerous ways to use this book; it is a book that you will come back to again and again.

PART 1

STORIES FROM
THE OLD TESTAMENT

CHAPTER 1

THE STORY OF CREATION: HAPPY BIRTHDAY, WORLD

> For in him all things were created: things in heaven and on earth, visible and invisible, whether thrones or powers or rulers or authorities; all things have been created through him and for him.
>
> - Colossians 1:16

THE STORY

In the beginning, God created the heavens and the earth. When God first created it, the earth was formless, empty, chaotic, completely covered in water, and dark, but it didn't stay that way for long. The

Spirit of God hovered over the waters over the waters and said, "Let there be light," and there was light. God saw that the light was good, and He separated the light from the darkness. He called the light "day," and He called the darkness "night."

On the second day, God said, "Let the waters separate, with those above being stored in a vault. He called the vault "sky." The Lord placed waters in the sky, and the rest he left on the earth's surface.

On the third day, God said, "Let the water under the sky be gathered into oceans, and let dry ground emerge," and it was so. God called the dry ground "land," and the gathered waters he called "seas." God liked what he saw and decided to build on it. "Let the land produce grasses, plants, and trees, all with seeds in them to repopulate themselves.

On the fourth day, God said, "Let there be lights in the sky to separate the day from the night, one season from the next, one year from another, and sacred days from ordinary days." God made two great lights—the sun to govern the day and the moon to govern the night. He also made the stars.

On the fifth day, God said, "Let the water teem with living creatures, and let birds fly in the sky." God blessed them, "Be fruitful and increase in number."

On the sixth day, God said, "Let the land produce living creatures," and God created the wild animals, livestock, and creepy-crawlies that crawl on the ground. Pleased with what he saw, God continued, "Now I will make humans to rule over all of creation." God then created people in His image.

On the seventh day, God observed that the heavens and the earth were successfully completed. God blessed the seventh day and declared it holy, for it marked the completion of His creation.

DEVOTIONAL THOUGHT

The book of Genesis is not a philosophy book. The writer does not give philosophical proof that God exists; the writer simply says that He does. If you don't want to take the Bible's word for it, though, you can look at the intricate details of the world around us. The Bible says that this intricate detail didn't happen by chance; it had a Creator. Someone or something had to set the world in motion. The Bible says that someone is God. (The Big Bang Theory and other scientific theories may suggest that it was gasses that combusted, but you don't have to choose between science and religion – perhaps science is telling the how, and the Bible is telling the who.)

Because the human mind cannot fully grasp the details of God, the Bible attempts to present aspects of God so that we can better understand Him. However, since the Bible does not completely show all aspects of God or provide proof beyond any doubt that He exists, some people choose not to believe that God exists. You must decide if you believe in a Supreme Being and, if you do, how that knowledge is going to affect your life.

QUESTIONS TO PONDER

- *As I begin this book, what is my belief about the existence of a Supreme Being?*

- *What does it mean to be made in God's image?*

- *When God created people to rule over all creation, He was trusting people to take good care of His creation. Do I take good care of the Earth? (Religious or not, it is in the best interest of all people for all people to take responsibility for the planet.)*

- *What can I do to better take care of the environment?*

PRAYER

"Almighty Father, I thank You for creating me in Your image and for forming this beautiful Earth. I am entrusted to care for Your creation, but I am unsure if I'm doing my best. Please guide me to nurture and flourish Your wonders. Amen."

CHAPTER 2

ADAM AND EVE: LIFE IS FULL OF CHOICES

> *This only have I found:*
> *God created mankind upright,*
> *but they have gone in search of many schemes."*
>
> *- Ecclesiastes 7:29*

THE STORY

On the sixth day of creation, the Lord God decided to make a creature that would oversee the other creatures on earth, a creature he called mankind. He formed Adam from the dust of the ground, breathed into his nostrils the breath of life, and placed the man with instructions in the Garden of Eden.

Then God said, "It is not good for the man to be alone, so He caused Adam to fall into a deep sleep, took one of his ribs, and created a woman. The man and the woman were both naked, and they felt no shame.

Adam excitedly showed Eve around the garden. When they got to the middle, he pointed to two unique trees, the Tree of Life and the Tree of Knowledge of Good and Evil. "God told me I was free to eat from any tree except these. He said that anyone who eats from the Tree of the Knowledge will die."

Several of the animals were crafty, but the serpent was craftiest. One day, finding Eve alone, he called, "Did God really say, 'You must not eat from any tree in the garden'?"

Eve repeated what Adam had told her. When she began describing the consequences of eating from the Tree of Knowledge, the serpent interrupted her, saying. "You will not die. God knows that if you eat it, you will be like Him, knowing good and evil." The serpent watched Eve stare at the fruit and coaxed, "It is not only beautiful, it has a taste like you have never experienced."

"But God said..."

"Don't you want to be smart like God?"

Seeing no harm in getting a little smarter, she bit into it. Eve had barely swallowed a bite, though, when Adam joined them. "Taste," Eve cooed, sticking a piece of forbidden fruit into his mouth.

No sooner had Adam swallowed it than he realized that he was naked. "Don't look at me!" he called, grabbing a large fig leaf and holding it in front of his waist.

"Keep your eyes off me, both of you," the woman demanded, putting her hands out to shield her body.

In the distance, they heard God coming. They hid, but when God mockingly called, "Where are you?" they knew they had been spotted. Adam confessed, "I heard you coming, and I was afraid because I was naked, so I hid."

God replied, "Who told you that you were naked? Have you eaten from the tree that I commanded you not to eat from?"

"The woman you put here with me—she gave me some fruit from the tree, and I ate it," Adam blurted.

God turned to Eve and said, "What is this you have done?"

Eve replied, "The serpent deceived me, and I ate."

The Lord God looked directly at the serpent, who, in turn, gave him an innocent, "Who me?" look.

God said to the serpent, "Because you have done this, you will henceforth crawl on your belly. I will put ill will between your offspring and hers – and hers will prevail."

Adam and Eve breathed a sigh of relief. They weren't dead, and it looked like God was winding down. However, He turned to Eve and said, "You will bear children – but not without great pain," and to Adam, he said, "Because you ate from the tree which I commanded you not to eat, you both will be exiled from the Eden, your days will be numbered, and you must toil the ground if you are to eat."

Although God punished Adam and Eve, He still loved them. In fact, God loved them so much that He sacrificed part of His creation to clothe them, giving them garments made of animal skins. Adam and Eve still loved the Lord, too, and they continued to worship him all the days of their lives.

DEVOTIONAL THOUGHT

Adam and Eve each decided to eat the forbidden fruit. Like them, we, too, must make decisions. Life is full of decisions; they range from "What color of socks should I wear?" to "Do I believe in a Greater Power?" Decisions come with consequences or, to say it more positively, with results. What we decide today can ripple across our lives for many days and years to come and can also affect those around us.

Many people want to make your decisions for you, and they will tell you what to think – which people to be friends with, which brands of goods to buy, and what religious beliefs to hold. Think things through; take responsibility for the decisions you make. Adam and Eve did not take responsibility for their decisions. When they got caught eating the forbidden fruit, Adam blamed Eve, and Eve blamed the snake, but God made it clear they were responsible for the choices they made. It's not always easy to take responsibility for our behavior, but it's the right thing to do.

QUESTIONS TO PONDER

- *What decisions have I made already today? (Hint: If you can't think of any, remember that choosing to read this article was a decision.)*

- *When I make a bad decision, what do I usually do? What should I do?*

- *Do parents still love us if we make bad decisions? Does God still love us?*

- *Why do parents/God punish us even if we are sorry for what we did?*

PRAYER

"Almighty Father, I seek Your wisdom and guidance as I make decisions each day. Help me choose the right path, and if I falter, lovingly redirect my steps toward Your will. Lead me with Your grace and understanding. Amen."

CHAPTER 3

CAIN AND ABEL: TAKE TIME TO REFLECT

> *By faith Abel brought God a better offering than Cain did. By faith he was commended as righteous, when God spoke well of his offerings. And by faith Abel still speaks, even though he is dead.*
>
> *- Hebrews 11:4*

THE STORY

Adam and Eve had many, many children. The first children to be born to them were sons. The younger son, Abel, was a shepherd, while his older brother, Cain, was a farmer. Adam and

Eve had taught the boys to respect God, and the two boys offered sacrifices to Him. One day when they offered their sacrifices, God gladly accepted Abel's sacrifice of the firstborn from his flock, but He did not accept Cain's gift of harvest fruits. This rejection was likely due to Cain keeping the very best for himself, but Cain was upset at being rejected.

God saw that Cain was angry, so he confronted him. "Why are you angry? If you do what is right, it will be accepted. If you refuse to obey, though, evil will fill your heart."

Cain sneered and waited for a chance to punish his brother for making him look bad. He found that chance one day. He invited his brother to go into one of his fields, and when Abel least expected it, Cain attacked him, killing him.

As Cain walked away from the crime scene, God called to him, "Where is your brother Abel?"

"How would I know?" Cain retorted. "Am I my brother's keeper?"

"Your brother's blood calls to me from the ground. From this day on, the soil will no longer yield crops to you. From this day on, you will be a restless wanderer, a fugitive, a tramp."

"Please don't do that, Lord. Whoever finds me will kill me."

"Not so," God assured him. "No one will dare to kill you, for I am making it known that if anyone harms you, their punishment will be seven times worse than yours." The Lord then put a mark on Cain, a mark so clear that everyone could tell it was him from a great distance away.

So, Cain went and lived in the land of Nod, east of Eden. He settled down with his wife and raised a son. Cain then went about building the first city, a town he named after his son, Enoch.

DEVOTIONAL THOUGHT

When hearing that Cain was sentenced to be a wanderer, a tramp who would go from town to town doing odd jobs to earn his keep, most people think that Cain was being punished. Cain, though, was being given yet another opportunity to turn his life around. God was giving him time to reflect and ponder what life was all about. (Sad to say, but Cain did not accept the life of a wanderer; instead, he settled down and built a city.)

Many people live with almost every minute of their day booked, and if there are a few minutes in their day that are not booked, they spend the time sitting mindlessly in front of the television set. They are almost robots, following a work-sleep-repeat pattern. Pausing to reflect wasn't just something Cain needed to do; it's something we all need to do! It's important to take time to ponder what we have accomplished, to count one's blessings, and to think about what one should do with one's life. By reflecting, you better understand other people and why they behave as they do, get a better understanding of yourself, think of goals, and ponder how to accomplish those goals.

Just as Cain was in control of his life, you are in charge of yours. By pausing to reflect at the end of each day, you can look at the decisions you have made. You can also plan what you are going to do tomorrow. Also, you can think about how blessed you are. By reflecting, you'll find that your life has meaning and purpose; you'll know where you are taking yourself and why you chose to go there.

QUESTIONS TO PONDER

- *If a loving God or a loving parent punishes me when I do wrong, what is the purpose of that punishment?*

- *What are some advantages reflecting offers me?*

- *Some people reflect by writing a journal or diary; others reflect by quiet meditation. Some write down what they are thankful for; others write thank-you notes. There are lots of ways to reflect. How do I plan to do it?*

PRAYER

"Almighty Father, I pause to reflect on my daily duties and ask if they are pleasing to You. I thank You for the blessings I didn't ask for and the loving discipline You provide when I fall short. Help me appreciate Your guidance. Amen."

CHAPTER 4

>>>>>>>>>>>>>>>>>>>✝<<<<<<<<<<<<<<<<<<<<

NOAH AND THE ARK: DON'T SETTLE FOR MEDIOCRITY

> 66
>
> *Whatever you do, work at it with all your heart, as working for the Lord, not for human masters,*
>
> *- Colossians 3:23*
>
> 99

THE STORY

>>>>>~~~~~<<<<<

As people began to populate the world, God observed that people were becoming more and more corrupt and that they were corrupting the entire world. Unwilling to settle for a corrupt world, God vowed to cleanse it. Out of all the people living, God found one man – and only one man, Noah, who was righteous and faithful. God called to Noah, "I am going to put an end to all people, for the earth is filled with violence because of them. I am surely going to cleanse the earth with water. You and you alone are living righteously, so I would like to spare you; I'll spare your wife, sons, and their wives as well. I am going to give you directions on how to build an ark. I want you to build it exactly as I say, stock it with food, and, right before the flood begins, I am going to send you two of each land animal – one male and one female - to load into the ark." Noah did exactly as God commanded, building the ark and loading it with the provisions and cargo God had specified. Once everyone and everything was in the ark, God sealed the door.

Rain fell for forty consecutive days, and the flood waters lifted the ark high, high above the ground. The water was so high that even the highest mountain was covered with water. After forty days, the rain ceased, but it would be months before the waters receded. After ten months, the tops of the mountains finally became visible.

Noah was curious about how much longer he would need to be cooped up in the ark, so forty days after the sighting of the mountain tops, he decided to send a raven to scout the area. He opened a window on the ark and let the raven out. The raven spread its wings and flew. The raven didn't see any dry land to roost in, but it did find carcasses and driftwood floating. Although the raven would occasionally fly around the ark, it settled happily into the life of a scavenger and did not return to nest in the ark.

Realizing the raven was not going to fulfill its mission of finding vegetation, Noah sent out a dove. The dove could not find anywhere fit to perch, so it flew back to Noah. Noah stuck his hand out the window, allowed the dove to land on it, and then brought the dove safely back into the ark.

Noah waited another week and then sent the dove on the vegetation-finding mission again. Noah released it in the morning, but this time, the dove did not return instantly. As morning turned to afternoon, Noah became worried about the dove, but his fears were relieved in the early evening when the dove returned with a freshly plucked olive leaf in its beak, proof the water had receded from the farmland. Noah welcomed the dove back.

Noah released the dove a third time a week later, and this time, the dove did not return. Realizing the dove had found vegetation upon which to thrive, Noah knew it was almost time to leave the ark. Although he wanted to go out immediately, he waited for God's permission. Finally, several days later, God said, "You may come out, you, your family, and all the animals. Be fruitful and multiply."

As Noah stepped out of the ark and onto solid ground for the first time in over a year, he looked upward to praise God, and up in the sky, he saw an arc of various colors. God said, "See the rainbow. The rainbow will be a reminder of the promise I am going to make with you and all the creatures of the earth – I will never again flood the earth." There has never been another world-wide flood ever again.

DEVOTIONAL THOUGHT

How dedicated are you to being your best? Are you, like the raven, willing to settle for mediocrity, or are you, like the dove, not satisfied until you find the best you can find and until you are the best you can be?

Being a raven is easy. For instance, you may be able to get a "C" on a test and not even study, but if you study, you could ace the test. Studying takes effort; are you willing to put in that effort?

Excellence does not come easy; you are going to have setbacks. The dove did not want to settle for mediocrity, and so it returned to the boat. On the second attempt, it found a sprig of hope, but not enough to call the mission accomplished. Finally, on the third attempt, it found the vegetation it was looking for. To continue to work for excellence paid off for the dove, and it does for us, too.

QUESTIONS TO PONDER

- *In what areas of my life am I like the raven, settling for the easy way when I should be like the dove, pushing to find the very best?*

- *What are some ways to ensure I push myself to be your best? (For instance, you could ask a friend to help hold you accountable.)*

- *The dove did not accomplish its mission the first two times, but it didn't give up, and it didn't settle for second best. If I'm not successful the first time, what can I do to make failure less likely the second time?*

PRAYER

"Almighty Father, I ask for the strength to strive for excellence and not settle for less. Help me resist the urge to give up easily and instead thrive in the purpose You've set for me. Guide me to accomplish Your mission with determination. Amen."

CHAPTER 5

>>>>>>>>>>>>>>>>>✝<<<<<<<<<<<<<<<<

THE TOWER OF BABEL: PRIDE, DIVERSITY, AND COOPERATION

> *Undoubtedly there are all sorts of languages in the world, yet none of them is without meaning.*
>
> *1 Corinthians 14:10*

THE STORY

In the days of early civilization, everyone spoke the same language. They continued with this language as they multiplied and settled onto the plains of Babylonia, part of modern-day Iraq. One day, a group of people said, "Let's build a grand city with a tower that reaches to the heavens; we will be famous."

Whereas most land had stone, the land they settled on had mud, mud that they could turn into brick and tar that they could use as mortar. Brick by brick, they began their ambitious building project. By carefully crafting uniform bricks and using scaffolding, pulleys, ramps, and other technology not common outside their group, the tower went higher and higher.

The Lord watched the construction and saw the people boasting about their accomplishment. They were giving glory to themselves and their building skills. The Lord listened and said, "This is not good. I will confuse their language so they will not understand each other."

When they no longer spoke the same language, they could not communicate well. They stopped building the city and scattered themselves across the earth. To this day, that spot is called Babel because the Lord confused the language of the world that day.

DEVOTIONAL THOUGHT

Pride is a healthy emotion. If you don't have any self-pride, you will not be confident. If your school doesn't have any pride, it will be a boring wasteland. Everyone and every institution needs pride. However, too much pride leads to arrogance. The people building the tower were arrogant. They expected all the other towns to look in awe at them.

When God saw how prideful they were, he decided to give them different languages. The people who spoke English gravitated toward each other and were very proud of English. Likewise, the people who spoke Russian gravitated toward each other and were very proud of Russia. (English and Russian are being used as examples to get the point across; English did not emerge until around the year 1000, and modern Russian did not exist until around 1700). Before long, the people who spoke one language thought they were superior to the people who spoke other languages; they thought their ways of saying and doing things were superior to the languages and ways of other people.

To be able to work together, people must not only overcome their language differences but also swallow their pride and find value in diversity and cooperation. We are living at a time where we can see that happening – in our local communities and the United Nations; we can also see that pride may ruin our cooperative efforts. To truly advance civilization, we must have a healthy dose of self-pride but also an appreciation for diversity and a desire for cooperation.

QUESTIONS TO PONDER

- *Do I have a healthy sense of pride? Do I lack self-esteem? Am I arrogant?*

- *How can I foster a healthy sense of pride?*

- *In what ways is diversity a good thing? Why should I seek diverse people to be friends with?*

- *How can I reach out and cooperate with people who are different from me?*

PRAYER

"Almighty Father, grant me the confidence to walk in Your purpose, but keep me humble. Let me be proud of what You accomplish through me, without falling into pride. Like the builders of Babel, correct me when I stray from Your path. Amen."

CHAPTER 6

ABRAHAM AND ISAAC: PRIORITIES MATTER

> 8 By faith Abraham, when called to go to a place he would later receive as his inheritance, obeyed and went, even though he did not know where he was going. 9 By faith he made his home in the promised land like a stranger in a foreign country; he lived in tents, as did Isaac and Jacob, who were heirs with him of the same promise. 10 For he was looking forward to the city with foundations, whose architect and builder is God. 11 And by faith even Sarah, who was past childbearing age, was enabled to bear children because she considered him faithful who had made the promise. 12 And so from this one man, and he as good as dead, came descendants as numerous as the stars in the sky and as countless as the sand on the seashore.
>
> - Hebrews 11:11-12

THE STORY

When he was 75 years old, Abraham had been told by God, "Leave your country behind you and go to the land I guide you. If you do, I will cause you to become the father of a great nation." Abraham demonstrated his trust in God by doing what God asked.

On the journey, God elaborated that Abraham's elderly wife, Sarah, would bear him a son, the start of the special lineage. As the years went by, Abraham and Sarah had doubts about this happening, but they ultimately kept their trust in God, and Sarah did bear a son.

They named their son Isaac, meaning "laughter," for Sarah had laughed – in shock, happiness, and skepticism - when God told her she was going to have a son.

By traveling to a strange land and by waiting patiently for a son, Abraham had passed the trust test, but before He further blessed him, God had another test for him – He wanted to determine if following Him was Abraham's top priority in life. Therefore, one day, God called to Abraham, "Abraham!"

Abraham heard and replied, "Here am I."

"Take your son, your only son, whom you love. Go to Moriah and offer him as a burnt sacrifice on the mountain which I show you."

The next morning, Abraham saddled his donkey, loaded it with wood, took two of his workers and his son, and started toward Moriah. On the third day, he found himself at the bottom of the mountain God intended him to use, and he asked his workers, "Stay at the bottom of the mountain with the donkey while Isaac and I go up there and worship; when we are done, we will come for you again." Abraham then laid the wood on his son's back, placed a torch and a knife in his own hands, and then together they started up the hill.

As they walked, Isaac asked, "You have the fire, and I have the wood, but where is the lamb for the burnt offering?"

"God himself will provide the lamb," Abraham said, continuing to lead the way up the hill.

When they got to the place God told him, Abraham built an altar, laid the wood on it, bound Isaac. and laid the obedient boy on top of the wood. He then took the knife into his hand and drew his arm back to slaughter his son, but the Lord called, "Abraham!"

Abraham kept his hand raised but paused to say, "Here am I."

"Do not lay your hand on the boy. I now know that you respect me above all, even your family, for you have not withheld your son from me."

Abraham lifted his eyes off Isaac. To his amazement, he saw a ram caught by its horns in a thicket. Abraham took the ram and offered it as a burnt offering.

As the offering burned, an angel called to Abraham, "God declares, because you have not withheld your only son, I will bless you; I will multiply your offspring, and they shall number like the stars of heaven and the sand on the seashore. Your offspring shall conquer his enemies, and all the nations of the earth will be blessed – because you obeyed my voice."

DEVOTIONAL THOUGHT

What is the most important thing in your life? Getting good grades? Earning money? Having friends? Your family? The Bible says that all of these should be secondary to following God.

Priorities dictate what we do and don't do in life. For instance, if your goal is to get good grades, before you do anything, you likely ask yourself, "Will doing this help me to get better grades?" If the answer is yes, then you'll do it, and if it is no, you won't. Similarly, since serving God and following His will are the top priorities in a Christian's life, then everything the Christian does is filtered through the question, "What would Jesus do?" If Jesus wouldn't do it, then the Christian doesn't do it.

Some people are both Christians and students; the two are not mutually exclusive. Although God is the Christian's top priority, the other things – getting good grades, earning money, having friends, and being with family - can still have a high place in one's life. There is nothing wrong with family bonds, having friends, and earning good grades; the Bible says they can't be the god of one's life.

- What is the most important thing in my life? What's second and third?

- How would my life be different if I changed a lower priority to my top priority?

- Will my current top priority today be the top priority for the rest of my life? Why or why not?

PRAYER

"Almighty Father, help me keep my priorities straight, placing You above all, just as Abraham did. Guide me to be a loving presence for my family, relatives, and friends, while ensuring my heart is fully devoted to You. Lead me in Your will always. Amen."

CHAPTER 7

JOSEPH AND THE COAT OF MANY COLORS: SIBLING RIVALRY IS REAL

> *Because the patriarchs were jealous of Joseph, they sold him as a slave into Egypt. But God was with him*
>
> *- Acts 7:9*

THE STORY

Abraham had two grandchildren from Isaac: Esau and Jacob. Jacob, in turn, had eleven sons, but his favorite was the youngest, Joseph. To show his love for Joseph, he made an ornate coat of many colors for Joseph to wear. When his brothers saw the coat, they were jealous; they were convinced their father loved Joseph the most, and they no longer spoke kindly to him.

Being the youngest, Joseph stayed home with his dad while his older brothers worked in the fields. One day, Jacob said to Joseph, "Go and see that all is well with your brothers, and then come back and report to me."

Joseph agreed to the task, put on his coat, and went walking down the road to where he thought they would be. When he got there, though, his brothers were not there – nor were the sheep. A man saw him looking around the fields and asked, "What are you looking for?"

"My brothers and their flocks. Do you have any idea of where they went?"

The man replied, "Those must be the shepherds I overheard. They said they were going to Dothan."

The man pointed; Joseph thanked him and headed down the road.

His brothers saw Joseph in his bright cloak coming their way.

"Here comes our little brother wearing his fancy coat," one brother said.

"He's going to tattle on us," another said. "He's going to see what we are doing and then report it back to dad."

"Let's kill him and throw him into a well; we can tell dad a ferocious animal ate him."

Reuben, the oldest brother, could see the murderous intent in his other brothers' eyes. He knew he couldn't stop his brothers, but he wanted to spare Joseph's life. Thinking he could come back to rescue Joseph, he suggested, "Let's not get his blood on our hands. Let's just put him in the well and let him starve to death." The other brothers agreed.

When Joseph approached his brothers, they stripped off the multi-colored robe and threw him in the well. They watched him land; the well was dry. They then sat down to enjoy their noon meal.

As they were eating, they saw a caravan of traders heading to Egypt. As Judah saw the immense treasure the traders had, he said to his brothers, "What do we gain if we kill our brother? Let's sell him."

When the merchants came closer, the brothers flagged them down. They pulled Joseph from the well and sold him for twenty shekels of silver. They then dipped the coat of many colors into goat's blood, took the coat home, and showed it to Jacob.

When Jacob saw it, he exclaimed, "It is my son's robe! An animal has torn him to pieces and devoured him." Joseph, though, was actually alive and well in Egypt. He had been sold to royalty, and he quickly rose to power.

When a famine came upon Jacob's family, elderly Jacob sent his remaining sons – including a new one – on trips to Egypt to buy food. Joseph recognized his brothers instantly, but he wanted to see if they had changed, so he didn't tell them who he was; after getting to know them and seeing how they had matured, he eventually confessed who he was, and he invited his father and brothers to settle in Egypt.

Jacob was hesitant to leave the Promised Land. However, God told him in a dream, "Go down to Egypt. I will make a great nation for you there, and I will surely bring you back again."

Having heard this, Jacob packed his belongings, and with his children, grandchildren, and everything he owned, he headed to Egypt.

He sent his son Judah to the palace to get specific directions of where in Egypt he was to settle. Judah got directions from Joseph, went back home, and then led Jacob and all of Jacob's family, livestock, and possessions into Egypt.

On the day Judah predicted they would arrive, Joseph was in his chariot waiting for his dad and brothers. Upon seeing his dad, Joseph clasped him, throwing his arms around him and weeping. It had been a long twenty years!

Have you ever been jealous? Jealousy can make a good person do bad things.

Jealousy stems from feeling inadequate. In the brothers' case, they were jealous because they sensed their dad loved Joseph more. The brothers also experienced envy, the desire of wishing that they had what Joseph had – a beautiful robe, a cushy role in the family, and their father's attention.

It's not a sin to feel jealous; everybody does. However, it is wrong to hurt someone simply because they have something you don't have. You can control how you react to jealousy. Joseph's brothers could have called a family meeting and shared with their dad how they felt about the different way he treated Joseph compared to them; instead, they chose to take their frustration out on Joseph. Be careful not to let jealousy get the best of you.

QUESTIONS TO PONDER

- *Am I jealous of anybody? Why or why not?*

- *Jacob played favorites. When I notice that a teacher or parent is playing favorites – lots of teachers have a "teacher's pet" - what can I do?*

- *If I happen to be someone's favorite and my peers are getting jealous of me, what options do I have?*

PRAYER

"Almighty Father, help me show kindness and love to my siblings, even when rivalry arises. Let them feel the same love and attention I receive from our parents. May they always know we are equal in their eyes, and may our bond grow stronger. Amen."

CHAPTER 8

BABY MOSES IN A BASKET: SOMEONE IS WATCHING OVER YOU

> *But the Lord is faithful, and he will strengthen you and protect you from the evil one.*
>
> *- 2 Thessalonians 3:3*

THE STORY

The Israelites and the Egyptians lived in Egypt in peace for many generations, but eventually, a pharaoh who cared nothing about Joseph's legacy came to power. He looked at how the Israelite population had grown and stated, "We must enslave these people. If war breaks out, they could join our enemy and fight against us."

The government put slave masters over the Israelites and made them work in hard conditions as farmers and masons. Although they were enslaved, the number of Israelites continued to grow rapidly. Seeing the Jewish population rising, Pharaoh declared that every Jewish male baby was to be thrown into the Nile River.

While the nation was under this decree, a married couple from the Jewish tribe of Levi had a son. The woman hid him for three months, but when she could no longer hide him, she knew she had to do something to save him. She got a papyrus basket and coated it with tar and pitch. One day, with the baby's older sister standing in the distance to watch, she placed the child in it and put the basket among the reeds along the bank of the Nile.

When Pharaoh's daughter went with her attendants to the river to bathe, she saw the basket. She instructed one of her servants to retrieve it for her. When she opened it, she saw the crying baby. "This is one of the Hebrew babies," she said, but she felt sorry for the child and did not drown it.

The sister of the baby then approached the princess and asked, "Shall I get one of the Hebrew women to nurse the baby for you?"

"Yes, please," the princess replied, so the girl went and got her mother.

The girl led her mother to the princess, who ordered, "Take this baby and nurse him for me, and I will pay you."

The baby's mother took him back to their home and nursed him. When the child grew older, she took him to Pharaoh's daughter, and he officially became the princess's son, and his mom became his nanny. The princess named him Moses, the Hebrew word for "draw out," saying, "I drew him out of the water."

DEVOTIONAL THOUGHT

Do you sometimes feel alone, feel that nobody cares? Baby Moses had that feeling. He was lying in a basket all alone. He did not realize that his sister was on a hill watching him. He did not realize that God was watching over him.

Although you may not always feel it, people are watching over you. Your parents, your teachers, your friends, your community, the government, and even God himself care about you. You may not always feel their presence, but they are looking out for your best interest. Sometimes, they will let you fall – parents let their toddlers fall all the time – because we learn from our failures. Moses's mother loved him dearly, but in Moses's mind, he was abandoned.

It's easy to forget that people care. Therefore, set aside time to remind yourself that people do care for you. For Christians, this mindfulness is often done with morning prayers, evening prayers, and/or mealtime prayers. For parents, it is often done by keeping pictures on their desks or in their wallets. Perhaps have your friends write down what they find special about you, and when you are feeling lonely or sad, pull out the list and remind yourself that they care and they see good things about you. Do whatever works for you, but keep reminders about you that you are loved.

QUESTIONS TO PONDER

- Who cares about my life?

- How can I remind myself that they care?

- Why do parents and teachers sometimes let me fail if they know I am going to fail?

PRAYER

"Almighty Father, I thank You for blessing me with family and friends who always watch over me. I am grateful for Your constant protection and the love of this caring community. Help me to also watch over those You love, as You have watched over me. Amen."

CHAPTER 9

MOSES AND THE BURNING BUSH: I DON'T ALWAYS FEEL QUALIFIED

> *Not that we are competent in ourselves to claim anything for ourselves, but our competence comes from God.*
>
> *- 2 Corinthians 3:5*

Moses spent the first 40 years of his life being raised as a prince in Egypt. One day, though, he saw an Egyptian beating a Hebrew; he went to the Hebrew's defense and accidentally killed the slave master. He buried the body and thought no one had seen him, but people had. When these people threatened to tell on him, he fled to Middin.

In Middin, he fell in love, got married, and became a shepherd for his father-in-law. One day, when he led his sheep to Mount Horeb, he saw a bush that was on fire – but it did not burn up. Curious, Moses decided to go over and examine the bush more closely. As he got closer, God called, "Moses! Moses!"

Moses said, "Here I am."

"Stop where you are. Remove your sandals, for you are on holy ground." Once Moses had obeyed, God continued, "I am the God of your father, the God of Abraham, Isaac, and Jacob." When Moses hid his face, God continued, "I have seen the misery of my people in Egypt. I have heard them crying, so I have come to rescue them and bring them into a land flowing with milk and honey. I want you to tell Pharaoh to let my people go."

Moses replied, "Who am I to go to Pharaoh?"

"I will be with you."

"Whom should I tell the Israelites has sent me? What is your name?"

God replied, "I am who I am. This is what you tell them, 'I Am has sent me to you.' My name is forever. Now, go, assemble the elders of Israel, and tell them what I plan to do."

"What if they do not listen to me? What if they call me a liar?"

God paused and asked, "What is that in your hand?"

"A staff."

"Throw it on the ground."

Moses threw it against the ground, and it became a snake; he ran from it in fear.

"Now, take it by the tail."

Moses grabbed the snake's tail, and it turned back into a staff. Seeing Moses still had doubts, God said, "Put your hand inside your cloak."

Moses did, and when he drew it out, his hand was as white as snow.

"Put it back in your cloak," God commanded.

Moses did. He then pulled it out, and it was restored.

"If they don't believe I sent you after seeing these things, take some water from the Nile and pour it on the ground; it will become blood. Rest assured; when they see this, they will believe I sent you."

"Lord, I have never been a good speaker. I stutter."

"Who gave humans their mouth? Is it not I, the Lord? I will help you speak, and I will teach you what to say."

"I don't mean to be rude, Lord, but please, send someone else."

The Lord became angry but said, "What about Aaron the Levite, your brother? We both know he can speak well. I will give the words to you to give to him; he will speak to the people for you. You, though, are in charge, not Aaron."

Moses took his wife and sons, put them on a donkey, grabbed his shepherd's staff, and started back for Egypt. Moses met Aaron along the way down to Egypt, and he told Aaron all that God had to say and about the signs that God had given him. Aaron believed what Moses had to say, and together, they headed down to Egypt.

DEVOTIONAL THOUGHT

Ever feel like you are being asked to do more than you are capable of doing? Parents and teachers often push us to our limits. They know that we are capable of things that we do not think we are capable of doing, and they ask us to do them. Just like Moses, our initial reaction is to say that we can't. Even when they assure us that they will help us, it is human nature to want to avoid such stressful moments.

In this case, God eventually agreed to let Aaron go with Moses. Moses thought that having Aaron along was reassuring, but God could foresee a sibling rivalry blooming (Numbers 12) and knew that Aaron could cave under peer pressure (Exodus 32). Moses and other Biblical heroes and heroines were real people, and, like people today, having complete trust in God is hard to do.

Are you being asked to do the seemingly impossible? If so, take it one step at a time. Remember that the person who gave you the task has confidence in you and is there if you need them; don't be afraid to ask for their help.

QUESTIONS TO PONDER

- *Do I like to take on tough challenges, or do I prefer to find easy problems? Why?*

- *How will I handle the next tough challenge I am asked to do?*

- *Moses had a stutter. Do I have a small flaw? How can I keep that flaw from holding me back from being all that I am capable of being?*

PRAYER

"Almighty Father, though I feel unqualified for Your purpose, I trust that You qualify those You call. I am ready to take on this challenge with You, but I ask for courage and confidence to overcome my flaws and become who You've called me to be. Amen."

CHAPTER 10

MOSES AND THE RED SEA: FINDING A WAY

> *This is what the Lord says—*
> *he who made a way through the sea,*
> *a path through the mighty waters,*
>
> *- Isaiah 43:16*

THE STORY

Pharaoh had been hesitant to let the Israelites leave Egypt, but, after Moses had brought about ten plagues onto his land, he had eventually given in to Moses's request. However, the Israelites had only been gone a short time before Pharaoh changed his mind about letting them leave. "What have I done?" he asked. "I have let the Israelites go, and we no longer have slaves." Realizing Egypt was going to suffer without the Hebrews being there, Pharaoh took his 600 best chariots, as well as many other chariots, and started after them. The Egyptians rapidly closed the gap between them and the fleeing Israelites.

The Israelites saw the Egyptians in the distance. Realizing they had the Red Sea in front of them and Pharaoh's army on all sides of them, they said to Moses, "Why did you bring us to the desert to die? We'd have been better off serving them in Egypt than dying here."

Moses replied, "Do not be afraid. The Egyptians you see today you will never see again. God will fight for you."

God asked Moses, "Why are they crying out to me? Tell them

to keep moving. Raise your staff, stretch your arms over the sea, watch it divide, and then go through the sea on dry ground."

Moses stretched out his hands as instructed, and the Lord drove the sea back with a strong east wind. With a wall of water on their left and another on their right, the Israelites crossed on dry land throughout the night.

The Egyptians saw the parted sea and decided to pursue the Israelites into it. When all of Pharaoh's army was in the water, the Lord jammed the chariots' wheels so the chariots could not be driven easily. Upon experiencing this, someone said, "Let's retreat. The Lord is fighting for them against us."

Meanwhile, as dawn was breaking, the Lord told Moses, "Stretch your hands over the sea so the waters flow over the Egyptians." Moses stretched out his hands, and the sea went back into its place.

When the Israelites saw the power of the Lord displayed against the Egyptians, they worshiped God and put their trust in him and his servant Moses.

DEVOTIONAL THOUGHT

With the Egyptians surrounding them on three sides and the Red Sea in front of them, it appeared that the Israelites were about to be slaughtered by Pharaoh's troops. They didn't see a way out, and they began to doubt whether they had been right to put their trust in God and his servant Moses.

God, though, hadn't led them that far to abandon them. He had a plan. Sometimes in life, we feel that we have done the right thing but run into a dead end. Things may look hopeless, but Christians know that God can make a way.

Even if you don't believe in God, you must admit that traditional ways to solve a problem do not work on every problem and that the average person does not think of bizarre ideas such as parting the sea. Also, you must admit that teachers and parents often see things very differently than we teens do. If your teachers or parents have said that a problem can be resolved and have asked you to take the first step, it may not be easy, but you should probably go ahead and take that first step; they see things differently than you do, and they likely have a plan.

QUESTIONS TO PONDER

- *If I had been an Israelite and had seen the Red Sea parted, would I have been brave enough to be among the first to walk across it? Why or why not?*

- *If I were Moses and saw the sea in front of me and Pharaoh's army on all sides of me, would I have been questioning God's plan? Why or why not?*

- *Have I ever had a situation that seemed impossible to resolve, but it got resolved? How did the successful idea get generated?*

- *Do I trust my parents? Your teachers? God? Why or why not?*

PRAYER

"Almighty Father, as I face the Red Sea of my life, grant me the courage to step forward in faith. Help me trust in You, the one true God, and move bravely while the enemies of doubt and fear stand at bay. Guide my steps. Amen."

CHAPTER 11

MOSES AND THE TEN COMMANDMENTS (MOSES AND THE GOLDEN CALF): SLIPPING BACK INTO OLD HABITS

> *9 All who make idols are nothing,*
> *and the things they treasure are worthless.*
> *Those who would speak up for them are blind;*
> *they are ignorant, to their own shame.*
> *10 Who shapes a god and casts an idol,*
> *which can profit nothing?*
>
> *- Isaiah 44:9-10*

THE STORY

After the Lord said to Moses, "Come up to me on the mountain. I will give you stone tablets with teachings and commandments that I have written for the people's instruction," Moses and his assistant Joshua set to go up the mountain. As they were leaving, Moses told the Israelites, "Wait here until we come back for you. Aaron and Hur are going to be here with you if you need anything."

Moses and Joshua were on the mountain for 40 days and 40 nights. While they were away, the people began to wonder if they were coming back. Eventually, the people went to Aaron and said, "Moses is likely dead. Make us gods who will go before us."

Aaron replied, "Bring me the gold earrings your wives and children are wearing."

Aaron took the earrings and put them into an idol cast in the shape of a calf. When the people saw the calf emerge, they said, "These are your gods, Israel." Aaron then built an altar in front of the calf and proclaimed, "Tomorrow, there will be a festival to the Lord."

The next day, the people rose early and sacrificed burnt offerings. They then sat to eat, drink, and party.

The Lord told Moses, "Go down the mountain to your people; they have become corrupt. They have bowed down to a golden calf and sacrificed to it, proclaiming it as the god who brought them out of Egypt."

Moses started down the mountains carrying in his hands two tables of the covenant law, inscribed front and back. When Moses saw the calf and the dancers performing around it, he was so angry he threw the tablets out of his hands, breaking them at the bottom of the mountain. He walked down the mountain, seized the calf, and tossed it into the fire.

As it burned, he turned to Aaron and said, "Why did you lead these people into such great sin."

"Please don't be angry with me," Aaron pleaded. "A mob came to me and said, 'Make us gods who will go before us,' so I told them to give me their gold. I threw it into the fire, and out came this calf."

Moses punished those who had participated in the worshiping of the golden calf and then the next day announced to the people, "As a group, you have committed a great sin. I will go up to the lord; perhaps I can make atonement for it."

Moses went back up the mountain. He took with him two stone tablets the size he had broken. On the mountain, he pleaded, "These are stubborn people. But forgive our evil and our sin, and accept us as your people."

"I will renew my covenant with my people of Israel," God stated, and then re-wrote the tablets for Moses. The Ten Commandments are as follows:

Do not worship any Gods before me.
Do not make or worship any idols.
Do not take the Lord's name in vain.
Remember the Sabbath and keep it holy.
Honor your parents.
Do not murder.
Do not commit adultery.
Do not steal.
Do not lie.
Do not covet.

DEVOTIONAL THOUGHT

We all have habits that bring us comfort. If I am guessing correctly, you follow a certain routine each morning. If you were to miss a step of that routine, things wouldn't feel right. We all have habits – many are good, some are bad.

The Israelites had habits, too. They had been slaves in

Egypt, and they had seen people worship Apis, a sacred bull. When they thought Moses was dead and that Aaron was their new leader, they craved an idol. They wanted something tangible. Moses had been tangible as God's servant, but they thought he was dead and gone, so they wanted something tangible they could see to give credit to. Bad habits are easy to fall back into.

It takes about three weeks of consciously doing something every day to make it a habit. If you have sat in the same pew at church for three weeks, chances are you are going to sit in that pew again this week. For Christians, this Biblical story serves as a reminder of how easy it is to get off the path of righteousness; for the secular person, this story serves as a reminder of why it is important to instill good habits; instill them now so that when the tough times come, you have them to fall back on.

QUESTIONS TO PONDER

- *Why do people fall into habits?*

- *What are some habits that I have? Try to think of at least two good ones and two bad ones.*

- *What is the worst habit that I have? What is a good habit I could replace it with? What steps will I take to instill the good habit?*

PRAYER

"Almighty Father, I know that old habits die hard, but I trust that You are watching over me. Please keep me from slipping into old, destructive patterns and help me find new, productive habits that glorify You. Guide me to replace the old with the new. Amen."

CHAPTER 12

ABRAHAM AND ISAAC: PRIORITIES MATTER

 *Do not conform to the pattern of this world, but be transformed by the renewing of your mind. Then you will be able to test and approve what God's will is—his good, pleasing and perfect will.*

- Romans 12:2

THE STORY

Having left Egypt, the Israelites headed to the Promised Land. Because the Jews had vacated the Promised Land over 400 years ago to go to Egypt, other peoples had settled upon it. Now that the Israelites were camping outside its border, God instructed Moses, "Send a leader from each of the twelve tribes to explore Canaan."

Moses assembled the team of spies and instructed, "I want you to explore the land from the desert to the mountains. Tell me about the land. Is the soil rich or poor? Are trees plentiful? Tell me about the people. Are they strong or weak? Are they many or few? If possible, bring back some fruit for us to sample."

The twelve spies were gone for forty days. When they came back, they showed fruit from the land and then stood in front of everyone and gave the following report: "The land you sent us is flowing in milk and honey; here is some of its fruit. However, the people who live there are strong. We even saw descendants of Anak, the giant, there. The cities have walls – very large walls."

The crowd murmured, but Caleb, another of the spies, said, "This is true. There are giants, and the walls are large, but we still should be more than able to conquer it."

All the other ten men except Joshua, who had spied the land, said to Caleb and the people, "We can't attack those people. They are too strong for us. We felt as small as grasshoppers, and we must have looked like grasshoppers to them."

The people of the assembly began to moan, "If only we had died in Egypt," "Why did the Lord have us walk all this way just to die by the sword," "They will kill us and take our children as plunder," and "Wouldn't it be best to go back to Egypt?"

Joshua spoke up, saying, "If the Lord is pleased with us, he will lead us into the land and will give it to us. The Lord is with us. Do not be afraid."

The assembly was turning into a lynch mob. People began talking about stoning Aaron and Moses. Suddenly, the glory of the Lord appeared in the meeting tent for all to see, and a voice said to Moses, "How long will these people treat me with contempt? They have seen miracles, signs, and wonders, and yet they do not believe. None of these people except Joshua and Caleb will enter this wonderful land; their children, the ones they thought were plunder, will conquer it. Tomorrow, set out toward the desert toward the Red Sea. You will wander for 40 years, one for each day of exploration, and then I will bring you back."

The Israelites did wander for 40 years, and only those under 20 years of age that day – except Caleb and Joshua, were around to cross into the Promised Land when they came full circle. Moses successfully led the people through the wilderness and back to the border, but even he passed away before the time came to enter. The next generation believed they could conquer the land with God's help, and God proved them right.

DEVOTIONAL THOUGHT

Have you ever heard the term "positive thinking"? Positive thinking does not mean thinking that you can do something automatically means that you can do it. Positive thinking is taking steps to be proactive, where you can make a difference and accept and make the most of what you cannot change. In other words, to set goals for oneself and to find the silver linings behind the dark clouds.

Moses, Joshua, and Caleb knew that the Israelites could claim the Promised Land. They knew they had the military; they knew God was going to assist them. The ten spies focused on the negative aspects, such as how big the natives stood, and concluded that the Israelites had no chance of success. Those with positive thinking focused on how equipped the Israelites were and believed they could not fail. If you believe you are going to fail, you will likely call it quits at the first setback. On the other hand, if you believe you are going to be successful, small setbacks are mere obstacles that must be overcome.

For Christians, this story points out that God will never ask believers to do something that He will not help them accomplish. For the secular person, it is a reminder that if negative thoughts enter our minds, we are apt to quit easily and not accept new challenges. Christian or non-Christian, having a positive outlook on life will tend to lead to greater happiness, a can-do spirit, and a willingness to take on new challenges.

QUESTIONS TO PONDER

- *Am I a positive thinker? When the world changes around me, do I welcome the change and find advantages in it?*

- *What are five things I could do to cultivate a positive mindset?*

- *Notice how fast the Israelites accepted the negative point of view. What makes negative thinking so easy for most people to accept?*

PRAYER

"Almighty Father, I understand the power of my thoughts, whether they lead to success or defeat, fear or faith. Help me not to doubt my abilities, but to trust in the strength You've placed within me, knowing it's greater than any challenge I face. Amen."

CHAPTER 13

THE WALLS OF JERICHO COME TUMBLING DOWN: DON'T WORRY ABOUT LOOKING FOOLISH IN FRONT OF OTHERS

 *Now faith is confidence in what we hope for and assurance about what we do not see.*

- Hebrews 11:1

Word about the advancing Israelites and their powerful God spread across Canaan, and the Canaanites walled themselves behind the protective walls of their respective cities. Jericho, the first city the Israelites encountered, was no exception. The city gates of Jericho were securely barred. No one went out; no one went in.

The Lord said to Joshua, "Look. I have delivered Jericho into your hands."

Joshua nodded in agreement.

"Here's what I want you to do. I want you to march around the city with all your armed men, seven priests each blowing a ram's horn, and other priests carrying the Ark of the Covenant, the gold-plated wooden chest that houses the two tables containing the Ten Commandments. Do this for six days. On the seventh day, I want you to march around it seven times with the priests blowing their horns. On that day, when you hear the priests give one long blast, have the people shout as loud as they can. The town walls will collapse, and your armed men can charge straight into town."

Joshua organized the procession. He had an armed guard march ahead of the priests, and a rear guard followed the Ark. He commanded the priests to blow their horns throughout the walk, but the warriors to say nothing. The procession walked around the city and then returned to camp. The parade was repeated five more times as the Lord instructed.

At dawn on the seventh day, they marched around the city again, except this time, they made a second, third, fourth, fifth, and sixth lap. On the seventh time around, the priests gave a loud blast, and Joshua exclaimed, "Shout! For the Lord has given you the city."

The warriors gave a loud shout, and the walls collapsed. The Israelites charged straight in and took the city easily.

DEVOTIONAL THOUGHT

The citizens of Jericho were terrified of the Israelites when the Israelites first surrounded their city. They expected the Israelites to attack, but instead, the Israelites simply marched around the city and then retreated to their camp. This happened a second day and then a third. By the fifth, sixth, and seventh day, the citizens' fear had turned to mockery. If you were a man of war in the Israelite army, this is not what you signed up for.

God often asks Christians to do things that make them appear foolish in front of other people. They trust Him, though, and they do them.

Secular leaders, too, make people do things that make them feel uneasy. For instance, you may be asked to stand in front of people and give a report. No one wants to look foolish in front of others, but being comfortable speaking in front of people is a valuable skill. Don't be afraid to look foolish; there is a reason behind the seemingly strange request – a meaning you may not realize for a long, long time.

QUESTIONS TO PONDER

- *Why did God instruct the Israelites to march around with just their horns sounding for six days and then give a shout on the seventh day?*

- *Why do most people dread looking foolish in public?*

- *Am I okay with looking foolish in front of others? Why or why not?*

PRAYER

"Almighty Father, help me follow the guidance of good leaders, even when I may not understand or look foolish. Remind me that obedience to Your will is more important than appearances. Give me the strength to trust in Your wisdom and direction. Amen."

CHAPTER 14

>>>>>>>>>>>>>>>>>>>>>>✝<<<<<<<<<<<<<<<<<<<<<<

ACHAN'S GREED: SMALL THINGS CAN MAKE BIG DIFFERENCES

> **"**
>
> *The greedy bring ruin to their households,*
> *but the one who hates bribes will live.*
>
> *- Proverbs 15:27*
>
> **"**

THE STORY

After capturing Jericho, the Israelites were very confident in their army. When Joshua received a report about Ai, the next city they needed to capture, the spies he sent said there was no need to send the whole army. Joshua listened and sent about 3,000 men – and they were routed.

Upon hearing the news of the defeat, gloom settled upon the Israelites. Joshua prayed, "Lord, how could you let this happen? I don't understand. Why did you bring us across the Jordan River just to have us killed? What will happen to your great name when we are wiped from the earth?"

"Israel has sinned," the Lord declared. "Someone has taken some of the things from Jericho that were to be devoted to me; they have stolen from me, they have lied, and they have put the items in their possession. This is why Israel cannot stand up to her enemies; this is why I will not be with you unless you destroy whoever among you disrespects me. Tell the people this is why, and I will tell them who the thief is in the morning."

God then gave instructions for finding the thief. He asked Joshua to group the people by tribe and have a representative of each tribe come forward. Each representative would draw a bead. The tribe that drew the colored bead would contain the culprit; the other tribes could breathe easy. Each clan in the designated tribe would send a representative to choose a bead. After the guilty clan was discovered, then a representative from each family would come forward. Once it was narrowed to a particular family, each male from the family would come up to draw. The male holding the colored bead would be the thief.

The next morning, Joshua did as God instructed. No one except the thief and his family knew who the guilty party was. Everyone looked at each other suspiciously; no one stepped forward to confess. The twelve tribes drew from the jar; the tribe of Judah was found guilty. The representative of the clans of Judah drew beads next, and Zerah was chosen. The families of Zerah drew beads next, and Zimri was singled out. Every male of Zimri's family selected a bead, and the lottery said the thief was Achan.

Realizing he was caught, Achan confessed, "It is true. When I saw beautiful robes, silver coins, and a gold bar in Jericho, I coveted them, and I took them rather than let them burn as a sacrifice to God. They are hidden in the ground inside my tent; the gold and silver are under the robes."

Joshua dispatched messengers to the tent who found the items just as described. They then took the things from the tent and brought them to Joshua, spreading them out before the Lord. "Do you know what you have done?" Joshua asked as he led Achan out of town to be executed.

DEVOTIONAL THOUGHT

If your initial reaction to Achan's crime was that the Lord was overreacting, your reaction is typical. We can rationalize the crime. In the nonbeliever's mind, those robes would just be going to waste if they were allowed to burn; in the believer's mind, God has created everything and is surely worthy of having nice things. Compared to all of the items that were to be sacrificed to God, only a minute fraction had not been sacrificed. That little bit, though, was noticeable to God. Also, the attitude of putting oneself before God was the beginning of a bad trend that needed to be nipped.

Do little things matter? They do. It may be tempting not to study for one test, but that attitude will likely begin to show up again and again – you need to nip bad habits as they begin. Those extra few minutes you spend tutoring a friend may not seem like much, but a few minutes over several days adds up; just six minutes per day is a half hour per five-day week. Little things – good things or bad things – do matter.

Pay attention to little things. If you can be trusted with small things, people will be more likely to trust you with larger things. Those extra few minutes you spent on studying may be getting one more question right, and that one more question may be the difference between a good grade and a great grade.

QUESTIONS TO PONDER

- *Why is it important to pay attention to details in most cases?*

- *What are some cases in which attention to detail is not needed?*

- *Am I a "big picture" person, a detail-oriented person, or both? What is the advantage of being both?*

PRAYER

"Almighty Father, teach me the importance of obedience and attention to detail. When Your instructions are clear, help me follow them wholeheartedly without taking shortcuts. Let my actions reflect my commitment to Your will and trust in Your perfect guidance. Amen."

CHAPTER 15

>>>>>>>>>>>>>>>>>>>>>✝<<<<<<<<<<<<<<<<<<<<<

SAMSON: IT'S NEVER TOO LATE TO DO THE RIGHT THING

If anyone, then, knows the good they ought to do and doesn't do it, it is sin for them.

- James 4:17

THE STORY

Having settled into the Promised Land, the twelve tribes of Israel formed a loose confederation with a judge to rule over them. When the people followed God's will, Israel prospered; when the people disobeyed God, he let her enemies overtake her. Israel would recognize how she had strayed, and turn back to the Lord, who then enabled Israel to overthrow her oppressors.

The Philistines had oppressed the Israelites for forty years when an angel came to Samson's mom and announced that her baby would become a judge and take the lead in overthrowing the Philistines. She believed what the angel said, and agreed to follow the instructions the angel gave - including to never cut a hair on his head.

Samson rose to the role of judge, but he was not interested in leading an army - he preferred to have a good time with his friends. Samson was incredibly strong physically, but he was very weak morally.

Although he had been called by God to fight the Philistines, and he had had a few personal run-ins with them, Samson had no motivation to lead an army against the Philistines. In fact, he, a Jewish man who was expected to marry a Jewish woman, found himself attracted to Philistine women. Although a lot of Philistine women impressed him, his woman of choice was Delilah.

The Philistine rulers saw the way he looked at her. They approached Delilah and said, "If you can find the secret of this Jewish leader's strength so we can subdue him, we'll give you 28 pounds of silver."

When she thought the time was right, Delilah then went to Samson and said, "Tell me about your strength and how you could be tied up and subdued."

"If I am tied up with seven fresh bowstrings that have never been dried, I'll be as weak as any other male."

The rulers brought her seven fresh bowstrings that had never been dried, and as he slept at her house one evening, she tied him up and then, as the Philistines hid in the room, called, "Samson, the Philistines are upon you." Samson sat up instantly, snapping the strings effortlessly.

"You lied to me, Samson," Delilah huffed. "Now, tell me how you can be tied."

"If I am tied securely with ropes that have never been used, I'll be as weak as any other male."

The next time Samson slept, Delilah tied him with never-used ropes. With the Philistines hidden in the room again, she called, "Samson, the Philistines are upon you!" Upon hearing this, Samson snapped the ropes off his arms.

"You are making a fool out of me," Delilah whined. "How can you say that you love me when you don't confide in me?"

She nagged him day after day until he finally broke down and confessed, "No razor has ever touched my head. If I were shaved, I would be as weak as any other man."

Convinced he had told her the truth, Delilah asked the Philistine rulers to come to her house while Samson slept. That night, as Samson slept reclining on her lap, the leaders brought the silver to her house for her and then shaved off Samson's seven braids.

"Samson, the Philistines are upon you," she called, waking him from his sleep. Samson awoke and saw the rulers; he tried to resist them, but his strength was gone. The rulers subdued him, gouged his eyes out, and took him to their capital in Gaza.

The rulers planned to offer a great sacrifice to their god, Dagon, claiming Dagon had delivered Samson to them. While waiting for the holiday, they bound Samson in bronze shackles and had him turn a millwheel as if he were a donkey. When the holiday arrived and the time was right, they sent for Samson to enter the arena.

As the blind brute entered the arena, about 3,000 men and women jeered him. No one noticed, but Samson's hair had grown back. Samson pretended to be weak, though, and asked the man who brought him from the prison to the arena, "Would you place me so I can lean against the pillars that support the temple?"

Once against the two central pillars, Samson prayed, "Lord, please, give me strength just once more." Then Samson braced himself between the two pillars, one on his left and one on his right. With a mighty shove, he broke both pillars, knocking down the temple and thereby wiping out the entire Philistine leadership team, fulfilling his destiny of leading in the overthrowing of the Philistines.

DEVOTIONAL THOUGHT

Have you wasted a talent? Samson wasted his. Samson was supposed to be a great leader and lead the overthrow of the Philistines. Samson, though, thought only of his own needs and did little for the people he was supposed to help. While he was eating, drinking, and being merry, his girlfriend, a Philistine, betrayed him, resulting in him going to prison to be held until he was publicly executed.

While he was in prison, though, he had time to do some soul-searching. As he walked in circles around the millwheel, he thought about his calling. As he walked, he realized it was not too late. He realized he could still lead the revolution by destroying the Philistine leadership.

Have you wasted your talent or your resources? (I admit I've made some pretty poor decisions in my life.) The good news is that you are still alive, and therefore, you still have a chance to make it right.

For religious people, this story reminds them that for as long as a person is alive, that person may still turn to God. Although human nature is to write off someone as a sinner forever, this story offers hope that even the most self-reliant, vile sinner can still turn to God. It is also a reminder that if you have wasted your God-given talent, you can still make a difference. God loves you, even if you make mistakes.

The Philistines intended to demoralize Samson by blinding him, putting him in prison, and treating him like a donkey. Samson, though, didn't give himself a pity party. Instead, he wisely took the time to acknowledge that his true power came from God and not his hair. He reflected on the gift of strength God had given him and how he had misused it. Having made God – not wine, women, and song – the focus of his life, he then sought to use his strength for God's glory.

QUESTIONS TO PONDER

- *Am I self-reliant? Do I rely on God? If God helps those who help themselves, can a person be both God-reliant and self-reliant?*

- *What talents and skills do I have? Am I using my talents and skills wisely?*

- *Samson took time to reflect on God, life, and his goals while in prison. Why is reflection important? Where can I take time daily to reflect?*

PRAYER

"Almighty Father, help me to keep doing the right thing, even when I fail. I trust You've placed in me all I need to fulfill Your purpose. Like Samson, though I may have strayed, thank You for giving me a way to accomplish what is right. Amen."

CHAPTER 16

>>>>>>>>>>>>>>>>>>>>✝<<<<<<<<<<<<<<<<<<<<

DAVID AND GOLIATH: OVERCOMING THE GIANTS IN OUR LIVES

> 66
>
> *or the Lord your God is the one who goes with you to fight for you against your enemies to give you victory.*
>
> *- Deuteronomy 20:4*
>
> 99

THE STORY

Thanks to the revolution begun by Samson, the Israelites broke free of the Philistines and became an independent nation again. The Philistines were not happy with that and sought to subdue the Israelites again.

One spring, when the Philistine Army invaded Israel, King Saul and the Israeli army went out to stop them, setting up defense on a hill. The Philistines settled into the hillside across from them. Each morning, the Israelites would go into their defensive positions, and the Philistines would go into theirs; no one dared to advance into the valley between them. No one, except Goliath and his shield bearer.

Goliath was a giant. Standing 11 feet 9 inches, he had a bronze helmet, 125-pound armor, and bronze greaves; he had a javelin on his back and carried a spear that had a 15-pound iron tip. Each day, Goliath shouted at the Israelites, "Choose a man to fight me. If he kills me, we will become your subjects; if I kill him, you will become our subjects and serve us." Upon hearing the Philistine's words, Saul and all the Israelites were dismayed and terrified.

One day, when Goliath stepped into the valley to make the challenge, a shepherd boy, David, who was delivering supplies to his brothers in the Israeli army, heard him and asked his brother, "Who is this uncircumcised Philistine that he should defy the armies of the living God?"

His brother retorted, "What's it to you?" but David wanted to know, so he asked someone else.

David's questioning was overheard and reported to King Saul, and Saul sent for him.

David went to the king's tent and said to the king, "Let no one lose heart on account of this Philistine; your servant will go and fight him."

King Saul looked at the ruby-faced youth and replied, "You are not able to go out against this Philistine and fight him; you are only a young man, and he has been a warrior from his youth."

David replied, "I can handle it. I'm a shepherd. I have killed lions and bears defending the sheep. The Lord who rescued me from the paw of the lion and the paw of the bear will rescue me from the hand of this Philistine."

Saul reluctantly agreed to let David go out to fight the giant, and he gave him his own tunic, helmet, armor, and sword. David tried walking in the king's garb, nearly stumbled, and concluded, "I can't wear these; I am not used to them."

David removed the king's armor and headed to a nearby stream behind the king's tent, chose five smooth stones from the stream, put them in the pouch of his shepherd's bag, and, with his sling in his hand, walked past the king's tent, past the

Israeli front line, down the hillside, and into the valley.

Seeing someone representing Israel coming, Goliath and his shield-bearer also moved to the center of the valley. Shocked at seeing that King Saul had sent a youth to face him, Goliath bellowed, "Am I a dog, that you come at me with sticks?" and he cursed David by his gods. "Come here," Goliath dared, "and I'll give your flesh to the birds and the wild animals!"

Continuing to walk toward Goliath, David replied, "You come against me with sword and spear and javelin, but I come against you in the name of the Lord."

David reached into his bag, took a stone, and slung it, striking Goliath on the forehead. The stone sank into Goliath's forehead, and he fell face down on the ground.

David ran up to the fallen, stunned giant, removed the Philistine's sword from its sheath, killed him, and cut off his head as both sides watched in amazement. With their hero dead, the Philistines began to shake in fear and turned to run. The Israelites rose from positions and chased the Philistines out of Israel.

DEVOTIONAL THOUGHT

Where do you put your trust? Goliath put his trust in the technology of his day. He had the best helmet, armor, greaves, and weapons available. He also put his trust in his own muscles and intelligence. David, though, put his trust in the Lord.

Putting his trust in the Lord, though, doesn't mean that David didn't do anything to prepare. David did a self-assessment and realized he had the skills to pull it off; he had faced lions and bears. David prepared for the worst; he only needed one stone to stun Goliath, but he brought five because Goliath had four brothers whom David suspected might come to get revenge for their brother's death. David wasn't afraid to accept human help - such as putting on the king's armor - because God sometimes works through other people, but when he realized his well-intentioned friends weren't giving him the advice that he needed, he didn't give in to peer pressure.

Everybody faces big, daunting tasks. Whatever the big tasks are in your life, know that with God, all things are possible. Those who rely on God know that although there may be setbacks, in the end, everything is going to work out; those who rely on God are optimistic even in the worst of times.

QUESTIONS TO PONDER

- *Everyone faces some problems or difficult people, figuratively evil giants in their lives. What are some giants that I am facing?*

- *When I face a giant, do I rely on my own skills, or do I put my trust in God?*

- *Why does God expect me to keep struggling until the tough time is over? How can I reconcile the wisdom of "let go and let God" with "God helps those who help themselves?"*

PRAYER

"Almighty Father, I thank You for helping me overcome the giants in my life, both seen and unseen. Though each day brings new challenges—impossible tasks, difficult people, or obstacles—I trust in Your strength and guidance to see me through. I place my faith in You. Amen."

CHAPTER 17

DAVID AND KING SAUL: RESPECT YOUR LEADERS AS PEOPLE- EVEN IF THEY MAKE BAD CHOICES

Show proper respect to everyone, love the family of believers, fear God, honor the emperor.

- 1 Peter 2:17

After David slayed Goliath, he became a hero among the Israelites. As he grew older, David became a very successful military leader and a family friend of the king and his children.   All was well until one day when David and King Saul were returning from a victorious battle, and the village women began calling, "Saul has killed his thousands," and then echoing, "David has killed his ten thousand." From that moment on, Saul became paranoid, thinking David would take over the kingdom.

Saul suffered from depression, and David often played his harp to soothe him. One day, at one of their sessions, in a fit of jealous rage, Saul tried to kill David by throwing a javelin at him. David realized he was not safe in the palace, and so he fled into the hills. Saul sought to capture David, and eventually, Saul received word that David and some of his friends were in the nearby wilderness. Upon hearing this, Saul took 3,000 men with him and began a manhunt.

As Saul and his troops scoured the area, Saul had to pause to relieve himself. He saw a cave where he could have privacy and went into it.

Saul didn't know it, but David and his men were inside the belly of the cave. One of David's friends saw Saul and said quietly to David, "Today is the day the Lord promised you, the day when you can do whatever you want to him."

While Saul was preoccupied, David snuck up behind Saul and cut the hem of Saul's robe. David considered doing much more, but he returned to his friends and said, "Saul is the Lord's anointed one. I cannot kill him, nor will I let you."

When Saul had finished relieving himself, he exited the cave. As the king walked away, David ran to the cave entrance, bowed, and said, "My lord and king." He rose and said, "Why do you listen to those who say that I am seeking to do you harm? Look what I have in my hand. It's the hem of your robe. I cut your robe, but I did not kill you – although I easily could have. Know that I am not evil; know that

I am not rebelling against you. The Lord may avenge me, but my hand will not be against you."

pon hearing this, Saul broke down and wept, asking, "Is that your voice, my dear friend, David." Through his tears, he said, "You are more righteous than I, for you have repaid my evil with good. May the Lord reward you for what you have done. I know now that you will certainly be king, and the kingdom will be in good hands."

David did not dare go down to Saul, fearing this might be a trap and knowing that even if it was not, Saul's mood could change in an instant. Saul, though, motioned for his men to retreat, and he and they went back to the palace.

DEVOTIONAL THOUGHT

What do you think of our national leaders? They are likely either too liberal or too conservative for you. You may agree with them on certain issues but believe they are off-target on other issues.

We may not agree with their politics, but we are to respect them. From a Christian point of view, they are ruling by the grace of God; if God were not willing to have them in charge, they would not be in charge. Does that mean that we must do everything they say? As long as it does not interfere with one's relationship with God, Christians are expected to follow the leader. David respected the office of the king and the man God had installed in it, but he certainly did not agree with the policies the king was following.

For a society to function, citizens must submit to those who are entrusted with leadership. Ideally, leadership is a privilege and a responsibility; the leader is responsible for the welfare of the people whom the leader governs. In a democratic society, if you don't like the direction the country is going, you can vote for a candidate who will make changes. Every voice – every vote matters

QUESTIONS TO PONDER

- *What do I think of the current leaders of my town? Of my country?*

- *Many people say the current politicians are immoral, corrupt, self-serving, and crooked. How can I show them respect for their position while not condoning all the wrongs they do?*

- *Can a person be patriotic and be a Christian?*

- *What are some changes I would like to see in the world? How can I help to bring those changes about?*

PRAYER

"Almighty Father, help me show respect to leaders, even when I don't agree with them. I trust that You have anointed them for their roles, and I will honor their guidance with respect and dedication. May I serve faithfully, knowing that You are in control. Amen."

CHAPTER 18

SOLOMON AND THE TWO MOTHERS: LOVE IS WILLING TO MAKE SACRIFICES

> *Children are a heritage from the Lord,*
> *offspring a reward from him.*
>
> *- Psalm 127:3*

THE STORY

King Saul died in battling the Philistines, and David became king of Israel. When David passed away, his son Solomon became king. As king, Solomon often had to resolve disputes among citizens. Solomon wisely asked the Lord for wisdom, and the Lord granted it to him. Stories of Solomon's wisdom were carried throughout the world. Here is one example:

Two women stood before the king. One woman introduced the case, saying, "This woman and I are housemates. We each had a baby boy within three days of each other. One night, her son died because she lay on him. She woke up, saw what she had done, and swapped her son for mine while I slept. The next morning, I got up to nurse my son – and discovered he was dead! On closer inspection, though, I noticed that it wasn't my son."

"The living child is mine," the second woman said. "The dead one is yours."

"You're a liar. The living child is mine."

King Solomon listened patiently as they argued back and forth. Finally, he said, "Bring me a sword."

The guards brought him a sword.

"Cut the living child in half," he ordered, "and give half to one woman and half to the other."

Upon hearing this, the real mother was moved into a panic because she loved her son. "Please, give her the living baby! Don't kill him!"

The other woman sneered, "Neither of us shall have him."

The king then gave his ruling, "Don't kill him; give him to the first woman. She is his mother."

When the people heard the verdict, they were in awe; they saw he had wisdom from God.

DEVOTIONAL THOUGHT

If you love someone or something, you will make sacrifices. The woman truly loved her son, and so she was willing to sacrifice her time with him so that he could live. Did she want to give him up? Certainly not; she was in court arguing for the right to keep him. However, she put the child's needs above her needs.

If you love your family, you are going to make sacrifices for the good of the family members. Perhaps you want to watch a particular show on television, but the rest of the family wants to watch something else, so you willingly watch their program. Likewise, family members are going to sacrifice for you. For instance, parents often give up fancy cars so that their children can have nice things.

For Christians, if you love God, you will sacrifice other things in his honor. For instance, you might want to play baseball during morning worship time, but because you love God, you will generally prioritize worship. Meanwhile, God so loved the world that He gave his only Son to die for humanity's sins and to offer eternal life. Love means sacrifice on our part; it means others are also sacrificing for us.

From a secular viewpoint, the story reminds us that we are all interconnected. Family cares for one another, and if one member is hurting, then all are hurting. Family members are compassionate.

QUESTIONS TO PONDER

- *What are some ways that my parents and siblings are sacrificing for me?*

- *What are some ways I am sacrificing for the good of the family?*

- *What does the sacrifice of Jesus mean to me?*

- *What is the difference between "wisdom" and "knowledge"? We go to school to learn knowledge; what are some ways I can increase in wisdom?*

PRAYER

"Almighty Father, I thank You for the sacrifice of Your Son for me. I am willing to make sacrifices for my family too. Help me stand down in disagreements if it brings peace and protects those I love, just as You have shown love through sacrifice. Amen."

CHAPTER 19

ELIJAH: THE FOOLISHNESS OF STEREOTYPES

> *But the Lord said to Samuel, "Do not consider his appearance or his height, for I have rejected him. The Lord does not look at the things people look at. People look at the outward appearance, but the Lord looks at the heart."*
>
> *- 1 Samuel 16:7*

THE STORY

Under the watchful eye of the Israelite King Ahab, the prophet Elijah had challenged the 450 prophets of Baal who sat at Queen Jezebel's table to a public contest to determine whose God was superior. The prophets of Baal would call to Baal to accept their bull as a sacrifice by bringing down fire from Heaven, and then Elijah would call upon the Lord to do the same.

On the day of the contest, the prophets of Baal had gone first, and nothing had happened. Elijah had gone second, and his sacrifice had been burned to a crisp. He then ordered the spectators to kill the prophets of Baal, which they did.

Once he got back to the palace, King Ahab told Queen Jezebel everything that had happened. Upon hearing the news that all 450 of her prophets had been killed, Jezebel swore she would take Elijah's life, and she sent a messenger to tell him so.

Elijah was afraid, and he fled for his life. Finally, exhausted, he sat under a broom bush. "Take my life, Lord," he pleaded and then fell asleep.

God didn't take his life, though, and when he awoke, he began a journey that lasted forty days and forty nights, bringing him to Mount Horeb. He found a cave in the mountain and went inside to camp for the night. Once he was inside, the Lord asked, "What are you doing here, Elijah?"

I have worked hard on your behalf. However, the Israelites have rejected your covenant, torn down your altars, and killed your prophets. Now, I am the only one left, and they are trying to kill me too."

The Lord replied, "Go outside of the cave and stand on the mountain. I am about to pass by."

Elijah stepped out of the cave. As he stood on the mountain, a powerful wind blew across the mountain and shattered rocks, but the Lord was not in the wind.

Following the wind was an earthquake, but the Lord was not in the earthquake either.

After the earthquake came a fire, but the Lord was not in the fire.

After the fire came an eerie silence and then a gentle whisper. When Elijah heard the sound of silence, he pulled his cloak to his face and stood at the mouth of the cave. The small voice then called, "What are you doing here, Elijah?"

Elijah repeated what he said before, "I have worked hard on your behalf. However, the Israelites have rejected your covenant, torn down your altars, and killed your prophets. Now, I am the only one left, and they are trying to kill me too."

"Elijah, there are 7,000 in Israel who have not bowed to Baal. Now, quit feeling sorry for yourself. I have work for you to do."

DEVOTIONAL THOUGHT

I am a big Dallas Cowboys football fan. Every game day, I wear my Dallas Cowboys t-shirt and my Dallas Cowboys hat. That's how I show my team loyalty.

Other people are fans, too, but they show their loyalty in different ways. Some sit and watch every game; some memorize statistics, and some babble about the team every chance they get. I have a stereotype of what a fan should do, and based on my definition, I may perceive that I am the only fan, but in reality, many others are fans, too.

Elijah had the same issue. He had a stereotype of what a God-fearing person looked like and how they would behave. Because no one was behaving just as he thought they should, he thought he was alone. In the story, God, whom most people stereotype as being brash and majestic, came as a small voice. God was saying to him, "Don't trust stereotypes; get to know the person."

As a Christian, sometimes it is easy to feel that no one else is a Christian. However, not all people who follow God are going to dress and act exactly like you do. What matters is what is in their heart.

The secular person, too, can fall into the trap of stereotypes. It is human nature to look at someone and make a snap judgment – it's part of the fight-or-flight response that our unconscious mind does for us while our conscious mind tries to gather facts. Although you cannot stop stereotypes from forming, you can override the stereotype. Get to know each person. Not all tall people like to play basketball; not all Germans like sweet-and-sour cabbage. You can't judge a book by its cover; you can't judge a person just by looking at them.

QUESTIONS TO PONDER

- *Why do people stereotype God? Why can't God be successfully stereotyped?*

- *Why do people stereotype other people? What are the benefits of stereotyping? What are the cons?*

- *Do I have any stereotypes that I believe are "facts" about certain races, genders, religions, professions, or socioeconomic statuses?*

- *How can I overcome stereotyping?*

PRAYER

"Almighty Father, help me not to make immediate judgments or stereotype others. Remind me that each person is uniquely created by You, knitted with care in their mother's womb. Teach me to see their special gifts and value them as individuals. Amen."

CHAPTER 20

JONAH AND THE GREAT FISH: DO IT NOW!

> *2 This is how we know that we love the children of God: by loving God and carrying out his commands. 3 In fact, this is love for God: to keep his commands. And his commands are not burdensome,*
>
> *- 1 John 5:2-3*

THE STORY

One day, God said to the prophet Jonah, "I want you to go to the city of Nineveh and warn the residents that I can no longer ignore the stench of their wickedness. Tell them that if it continues, I will destroy their great city."

Jonah, though, had no desire to preach to the Ninevehites – perhaps he was scared that he would be beaten up for being a Jewish man telling a gentile people that they were sinners, or perhaps he didn't want God to spare them. Whatever his motive, he went as fast as he could in the opposite direction. He went to Joppa, where he found a boat at the port. He paid his fare, boarded, and then went below deck to hide.

The boat set sail for Tarshish. Jonah may have thought he was hiding, but God knew exactly where he was. God sent a great wind followed by a violent storm, a storm so violent that the ship was on the verge of breaking apart.

The sailors were experienced seamen, but even they were terrified. They each began to call to their own god to take control of the storm, but the storm raged on. In desperation, they threw the cargo overboard, lightening the ship.

As the storm raged, the captain went below deck, where he saw Jonah sleeping. "How can you sleep? Wake up! We're in the middle of a terrible storm. Call to your god! Maybe he is more powerful than this storm and will have mercy on us."

As the storm continued to rage, the sailors decided to draw straws to find out who was responsible for the calamity. When Jonah, who had joined the others in the pouring rain on deck, drew the short straw, they asked, "Who is so upset with you that he brought this storm upon us? Who are you? Where are you from? What is your background? What are you doing on this boat?"

Jonah proclaimed, "I am a Jew. I am running from God, the creator, the maker of the sea and the dry land."

"What have you done?" they gasped.

Jonah told them.

As Jonah talked, the sea was getting rougher by the minute. As he finished his story, the sailors asked, "What should we do to you to make the sea calm down?"

Jonah didn't even have to think. "Throw me into the sea, and it will calm down. It's my fault this storm has come."

The sailors had no intention of losing any lives, so they tried to row back to land. The sea, though, got wilder and wilder.

"Throw me into the sea, and it will calm down," Jonah repeated.

The sailors gathered around him. They looked up to Heaven and called, "Please, God, do not kill us for taking this man's life. Do not hold us accountable for killing him." They then took Jonah and threw him overboard.

As Jonah hit the water, the sea suddenly stopped raging. The sailors were horrified – and amazed – at this. That day, they worshiped the Lord.

Meanwhile, as Jonah sank into the water, a huge fish swallowed Jonah. Jonah, too, was horrified and amazed. He began singing songs and praising God. He repented of his sin. As he sang and prayed, the fish swam, and, on the third day, it vomited him up on a beach outside Nineveh. Jonah knew God's spirit was with him, and so, full of confidence, he went into the city and began to preach as God had instructed him to do.

DEVOTIONAL THOUGHT

Sooner or later, all of us must do something that we don't want to do but that we need to do because it is the right thing to do. In Jonah's case, it was going to the city of Nineveh to preach. In your case, it may be studying for a test, confessing to someone you broke something of theirs, or cleaning out the fish tank.

It's natural to procrastinate. Most of us can readily find things to do to fill the time that we should have spent doing that intimidating task. Although we can stall and put it off, eventually, we are going to have to do it or suffer the consequences of not doing it.

Jonah thought that he could fool God. He thought that out of the millions of people in the world and the thousands of spaces to hide that God would never find him hiding inside a boat. Jonah believed that by hiding so God couldn't find him, he wouldn't have to do the unpleasant task God wanted him to do He was wrong. No one is insignificant in God's eyes, and God knew exactly where he was. Sometimes, it is tempting to believe that we are so insignificant that what we say or do does not matter, but that is certainly not the case. What you do matters. Do the right thing – today and every day – no matter how difficult it might be.

QUESTIONS TO PONDER

- *What problems am I trying to run away from?*

- *Why do I procrastinate?*

- *What are some ways that I can "just do it"? (For instance, one could take an intimidating task and break it into manageable chunks with realistic deadlines.)*

PRAYER

"Almighty Father, I thank You that Your commands are not burdensome. Help me to respond to Your call without delay, knowing there is no escaping Your purpose for my life. Following You is not a choice of yes or no, but of when. Let it be now. Amen."

CHAPTER 21

JONAH AND THE PLANT: FIRST WORLD PROBLEMS

> *The rabble with them began to crave other food, and again the Israelites started wailing and said, "If only we had meat to eat!*
>
> *- Numbers 11:4*

THE STORY

After Jonah was vomited from the fish, he went to Nineveh and preached just as God had commanded him. Jonah despised the Ninevites, and it was with sadistic glee that he told them that God was going to rain destruction upon them in 40 days because of how unrighteous they were.

On the big day, Jonah made himself a shelter east of the city. Jonah watched and waited, but nothing happened. Jonah began to sense that God had relented, that the Ninevites had repented, and God had forgiven them. "Isn't this what I said would happen, Lord?" Jonah sighed, "You are a loving God, a God who relents from sending calamity."

The day wasn't over, though, so Jonah kept watching and hoping that his prophecy of destruction would come true. God saw him watching and provided a leafy plant, making it grow to give Jonah shade from the heat. Jonah was grateful for the plant.

The next morning at dawn, the Lord provided a worm which chewed into the plant, causing it to wither. He then sent a scorching wind to complement the blazing sun. Jonah, who was still hoping to see the destruction of Nineveh, was miserable, and so he called, "Why don't you just kill me?"

"Is it right for you to be angry about the plant?" God asked.

"It is!" Jonah snapped. "I'm so angry; I wish I were dead."

"You have been very concerned about this plant, but you did not raise it; it simply sprang up one day and died the next. If you have concern for this plant, is it wrong for me to have concern for the city of Nineveh with its 120,000 residents who are in spiritual darkness – and also their animals?"

DEVOTIONAL THOUGHT

Do you get frustrated when you can't find the remote to change the television channel? Do you get irritated when you have to stand in line for a few seconds before being handed a piping-hot school lunch? Do you get angry when a player on your favorite sports team makes a mistake? Lots of people do!

Those are first-world problems. We don't have to deal with third-world problems such as where our next meal is coming from, whether there will be clean drinking water, and whether we will live another day. Whereas we in first-world countries get frustrated with missing remotes, having to wait in line for a few seconds, and watching our favorite team stumble, third-world countries consider these frustrating events to be trivial. People in third-world countries are focused on issues of daily survival, something people in first-world countries take for granted.

Jonah had a first-world problem; his shade had disappeared. The people in Nineveh had third-world problems, including concerns for their spiritual health and their physical well-being. In our first-world culture, it is easy to become like Jonah, focus on our own needs, and ignore the third-world needs of those around us.

QUESTIONS TO PONDER

- *What things get you upset? Write a list, and then ponder which of these, if any, are really worth being upset over.*

- *Jonah had been asked to make a difference in the lives of people that he did not like. Would I be willing to make the world better for people that I do not like?*

- *The story ends with a "rhetorical question," a question that is asked, but the answer is so obvious that no one bothers to answer it. How would I answer it – the question was, "If you have concern for this plant, is it wrong for me to have concern for the city of Nineveh" - if I were to answer it?*

PRAYER

"Almighty Father, when I face trivial problems, help me not to grumble like the Israelites did for meat when they had manna. Open my eyes to see and appreciate what You've already provided. Help me focus my energy on what truly matters. Amen."

CHAPTER 22

>>>>>>>>>>>>>>>>>>>>✝<<<<<<<<<<<<<<<<<<<

JOB: IS YOUR LOVE CONDITIONAL?

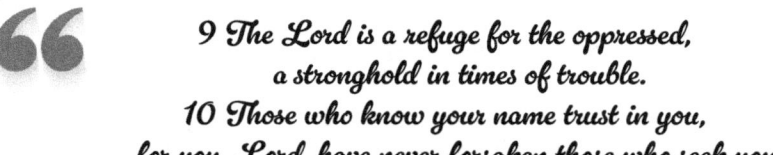

> **9** The Lord is a refuge for the oppressed,
> a stronghold in times of trouble.
> **10** Those who know your name trust in you,
> for you, Lord, have never forsaken those who seek you.
>
> - Psalm 9:9-10

THE STORY

Job was a model citizen in the land of Uz; he feared God and stayed away from evil. He was known as the greatest man among all people for another reason, too – he was rich. He had 7,000 sheep, 3,000 camels, 500 teams of oxen, 500 donkeys, and a vast number of servants. His pride and joy, though, were his seven sons and three daughters.

One day, when the angels presented themselves to the Lord, Satan came with them. Satan stated, "It's no wonder Job likes you. You protect him and his family. You bless the work of his hands and thereby multiply his flocks and herds. Take away the protection and the blessing, and I bet he won't praise you anymore."

The Lord replied, "I'll tell you what; everything he has is now in your power; do not touch a hair on Job himself, though."

Satan then disappeared to create havoc in Job's life.

The Lord replied, "I'll tell you what; everything he has is now in your power; do not touch a hair on Job himself, though."

Satan then disappeared to create havoc in Job's life.

One day later, a messenger said to Job, "Your enemies attacked, stole your oxen and donkeys, and killed all of your servants in the fields except me."

While he was still discussing the attack, another messenger ran in and said, "Fire fell from the heavens and burned up the sheep and all who worked with them except me."

Before he could go into detail, another messenger came and announced, "Desert nomads raided the camels, taking all of them and killing all of the workers except me."

Another messenger rushed in before he finished reporting and announced, "Your sons and daughters were at your oldest son's house feasting when a mighty wind caused the house to fall in on them. I alone lived through it."

Hearing this, Job rose, ripped his robe, and shaved his head. He fell to the ground to worship God, saying, "God giveth, and God taketh away; may the name of God be praised."

Satan was frustrated, but he showed up again in God's court. God greeted him, "Have you seen Job lately? He has nothing, but he still worships me."

Satan was ready with his request, "Of course he worships you; you keep him safe. Take away his health, though, and he will surely curse you."

God replied, "You may take away his health, but spare his life."

Upon leaving God's presence, Satan covered Job with boils from the top of his head to the bottom of his feet.

His wife saw Job scraping his skin with broken pottery and advised, "Enough with your integrity; curse God and die."

"You talk foolishness," Job replied. "Should we only accept good things and never the bad?"

Job's friends also came to advise him and to discuss why bad things happen to good people. Job listened but kept praising God; he even prayed for his friends.

Because Job remained steadfast through these times of trial, the Lord gave him twice as much as he had before. Job even sired more children – seven sons and three daughters, the three most beautiful girls in the entire world. Job then lived 140 years longer, watching his children grow to adulthood and their children's children as well.

DEVOTIONAL THOUGHT

Is your love for God conditional? Do you love God as long as he blesses you? Would you love God if he didn't bless you? Do you love God as long as he helps you? Would you love God if he let you flounder to work through a problem for yourself? Satan believes it is easy to love God – or at least be apathetic toward God - when God is blessing you, protecting you, and looking out for you. Job was right; everything we have is a gift from God. He gave it; he can take it away. Our love for God should be unconditional.

Is your love for your parents conditional? Do you love them "as long as they do XYZ," or do you love them unconditionally? Do you truly love your siblings, even if they take your toys? Later in life, you may find a mate. Will you love that person unconditionally, or will you put conditions on your love? If we truly love somebody, we don't put conditions on our love.

QUESTIONS TO PONDER

- *Why does God allow bad things to happen to good people?*

- *Do I believe that God blesses those who love him? Are those blessings always financial, or are there other forms of blessings as well?*

- *Do I love my family members unconditionally? Why or why not?*

PRAYER

"Almighty Father, I know that You sometimes allow bad things to happen to good people. Help me to see this as a blessing, a chance to discover the depth of my love for You. Teach me to love You unconditionally, not just in good times, but always. Amen."

CHAPTER 23

DANIEL AND THE LION'S DEN: STANDING FOR YOUR PRINCIPLES NO MATTER WHAT

> *Be on your guard; stand firm in the faith; be courageous; be strong.*
>
> *- 1 Corinthians 16:13*

THE STORY

Daniel was a Jewish boy living in Jerusalem when he and many others were taken prisoner by the Babylonian army and carried off to Babylon. The Babylonians realized that Daniel was smart, and they provided him and other exceptionally bright Jewish boys with a three-year course in Babylonian culture and then placed them in government positions.

When Babylon fell to Persia, the Persians also realized Daniel's talent for governing. The Persian king divided Babylon into 120 counties and appointed a ruler over each county. Daniel and two other administrators were tasked with ruling over these 120 counties, but Daniel was so good at it that the Persians soon decided to place him over the whole empire.

When the 120 rulers and the two administrators heard of the king's plan for Daniel, they sought to halt it by finding something Daniel did poorly. They couldn't find anything. Daniel was fair, responsible, loyal, and trustworthy; everything one would want in a governing official. They were about to conclude there was nothing they could do to turn the king against Daniel, but then they remembered that Daniel was a Jew, and even though he was miles from Israel, he still practiced the Jewish religion as best as he could. Working together, they came up with a plan that would make Daniel either violate his religion or break the law – making him either a terrible role model or a criminal.

These rulers and administrators then went to the king and declared, "Long live the king! Sire, we are all in agreement – we want to celebrate you. We propose that you make a decree that you be given glory and that for the next thirty days, anyone who prays to anyone or anything but you will be tossed into the lion's den." The king liked the idea, so they stuck a scroll in front of him and said, "Sign this idea into law, an official law that cannot be revoked." With everybody staring at him, the king signed the decree into law, a law that not even he could change. As he finished signing, the room burst into cheers of, "Long live the king."

The administrators were quick to make sure that Daniel knew about the law, knowing that he prayed three times per day; they wanted to make sure Daniel could not deny knowing about the law. Despite hearing of the law, Daniel went to his home, knelt in his upstairs window facing Jerusalem, and prayed as he always did, asking for God's help in governing. The administrators were watching for him from below, and when they saw him, they went to the king and asked, "Didn't you sign a law saying that anyone who prays to anyone except you will be thrown into the lions' den?"

"I did," the king affirmed. "It is an official law that not even I can revoke."

"Sire, that man Daniel, one of the captives from Israel, is knowingly ignoring the law and disrespecting you; he is praying to his God."

The king didn't want to kill Daniel and spent the next several hours looking for a loophole. Finding none, he gave the orders that Daniel be arrested and thrown to the lions. As Daniel was being led to the lion's den, the king said, "May your God, whom you faithfully serve, rescue you."

The guards then placed Daniel in the lions' den and placed a boulder in front of the entrance. The king then placed the royal seal on the stone, and the nobles placed theirs as well; if anyone attempted to rescue Daniel, the seals would have to be broken.

The king returned to his palace, sickened by what he had done. He couldn't eat or sleep. The next morning, he rushed to the lions' den and called, "Daniel, did your God save you?"

Daniel answered, "Long live the king! God sent his angels who shut the lions' mouths so they would not hurt me."

The king was delighted and asked that Daniel be lifted immediately from the den. Once he was up, the king examined him; not a scratch was on him. The king then ordered that the men who had plotted against Daniel be arrested. He had them and their family members lowered into the lions' den; the lions leaped on them, tearing them apart before they ever touched the den's floor.

The king then sent a message to every nation in every known language, declaring, "Everyone in my kingdom should tremble with fear before the God of Daniel, for He is the living God, and He will endure forever. He rescues and saves people; he rescued Daniel from the power of the lions."

From that day on, Daniel and his God were highly respected, and no one tried to usurp Daniel's rule.

DEVOTIONAL THOUGHT

Have you ever been teased for what you think or what you do? If you haven't, rest assured that day is coming. When experiencing such teasing, it is easy to deny what one believes and to do what the crowd wants one to do.

Daniel could have taken the easy way out. He could have scrapped his prayer life for thirty days. To Daniel, though, his time praying was so important that he wouldn't give it up; he valued his time praying that much.

When we have principles, we, too, need to be firm in our convictions. We may be teased for them; we may suffer for them. However, when others see us being true to our principles, just like the king saw Daniel was true to his principles, they develop a respect for us as a person, and, just like the king, they are often persuaded by our ardent example.

QUESTIONS TO PONDER

- *What principles do I have?*

- *How committed am I to those principles? Why?*

- *Sooner or later, my principles will come under attack. Can I verbally express my reasons for having those principles?*

PRAYER

"Almighty Father, strengthen my commitment to my principles, even when facing adversaries. Help me stand firm and fearless, especially when my faith is tested. Remind me that just as You shut the mouths of lions, You protect those who trust in You. Amen."

CHAPTER 24

>>>>>>>>>>>>>>>>>>>>>✝<<<<<<<<<<<<<<<<<<<<<

ESTHER: HAVE COURAGE TO BE YOURSELF

> 66
>
> *without being frightened in any way by those who oppose you. This is a sign to them that they will be destroyed, but that you will be saved—and that by God.*
>
> *- Philippians 1:28*
> 99

THE STORY

Esther was a beautiful Jewish girl who was being raised by her uncle, a high-ranking steward at the Persian king's palace. When her uncle became aware the king had requested all beautiful virgins to be rounded up and presented to him so he could select a wife, he made sure Esther was one of the candidates. The king was so impressed with her beauty that he married her, making her queen, without even taking time to get to know her.

Many Persians were prejudiced against the Jews, so since the king didn't ask, she did not reveal that she was Jewish. In fact, Haman, an evil noble who served as prime minister, secretly planned to have all the Jews executed.

Esther became aware of the plot when she heard Haman say to the king, "As you know, there are certain people who do not follow our customs; it is not in your interest to tolerate them. Let a decree be issued to destroy them. If you will, I'll give you a gift of silver."

The king handed Haman his signet ring so Haman could write the order and put the king's seal on it. "Keep the money and do with the people as you please. I need loyal subjects." Haman then sent dispatches throughout the kingdom in the name of the king that all

Jews – all Jews, including women and children – were to be killed on the thirteenth of the month and that their possessions were to be plundered.

Esther heard of the plot and sought to stop it. A few days before the slaughter was to take place, she held a banquet. The king was enjoying himself and stated, "Queen Esther, what would you like? Ask, and it will be given. Up to half the kingdom will be granted."

Esther replied, "Grant me my life."
The king was puzzled.

Esther continued, "My people are to be destroyed, killed, and annihilated."

The king couldn't believe what he was hearing. "Who would do such a thing?"

"An adversary and an enemy, the vile Haman."

The king now realized that his wife was Jewish. He was furious that he had been manipulated by Haman and had his guards arrest Haman. Haman pleaded with the queen for mercy, but she had him led away.

"I cannot rescind the order," the king said. "I wish I could, but it is written so that not even I can."

Esther replied, "Then let me and my people arm ourselves to protect ourselves from whoever seeks to kill us."

The king then issued an edict that granted the Jews the right to destroy, kill, and annihilate anyone who sought to attack them on the thirteenth day of the month, and he gave them the right to their attacker's property. The message was sealed with the king's ring and then sent by mounted couriers on the fastest horses the king had.

The Jews greeted the king's announcement with great joy. God, working through Esther, had saved them. To remember this special event in their history, the Feast of Purim was established and is celebrated to this day.

DEVOTIONAL THOUGHT

Just as in Esther's day, we all wear figurative masks. That is, we all hide parts of ourselves that we do not want others to know. Esther hid the fact that she was Jewish. The Israelites had been carried off from Israel to Babylon; Babylon, in turn, had been conquered by Persia. Persians were very prejudiced against Jews, so she kept the fact that she was Jewish to herself.

Esther, though, had worked her way into the king's court. She had started as one of over a thousand girls the king recruited for his harem, and by using her wit, charm, and beauty, she succeeded in being the one he chose to be queen. Life was good. She had bloomed where she was planted. She never dreamed God would have a use for her.

It doesn't matter what profession you enter; God is going to be able to use you for His glory. Esther made a difference in the lives of a nation; you may make a difference in only a life or two. Like Esther, you may not make a big deal about your religious beliefs, but sooner or later, they will come into play.

The same is true with the principles of nonbelievers as well. For instance, perhaps you have strong feelings about the environment, but you don't go around publicly making a big deal about your beliefs. Sooner or later, the people you hang around or the company you work for are going to face an environmental issue, and you will have to share your beliefs if you are to remain true to those beliefs.

QUESTIONS TO PONDER

- *Why do people hesitate to talk about their religious beliefs with others?*

- *Is being the "true me" important?*

- *What important things or secrets about myself do I keep away from most people?*

- *How can I let my friends get to know the real me better?*

PRAYER

"Almighty Father, I come to You, alone and without help, trusting in Your power. My danger is near, but I ask for the courage of Esther, who bravely approached the king, risking her life. Help me be as fearless and bold in the face of trials. Amen."

CHAPTER 25

>>>>>>>>>>>>>>>>>>>>>✝<<<<<<<<<<<<<<<<<<<<

NEHEMIAH REBUILDS THE TEMPLE AND JERUSALEM: LET SCOFFERS SCOFF

> " Look, you scoffers,
> wonder and perish,
> for I am going to do something in your days
> that you would never believe,
> even if someone told you."
>
> - Acts 13:41

Nehemiah was a cupbearer in the Persian king's court. He and his brother, Hanani, were descendants of Jews who had been taken from Jerusalem during the Babylonian captivity. Although Nehemiah had chosen to remain in Persia, his brother had returned to Israel. One day, his brother came to the palace, and the conversation turned to their native land.

"Those who were not taken into exile still live on the land, but they are in great, great trouble. Others bully them, and Jerusalem itself is still in shambles after all these years; the wall of the city has never been restored."

Upon hearing this, Nehemiah mourned, fasted, and prayed.

When Nehemiah reported for work, the king noticed a great change in Nehemiah. "What is troubling you?" the king asked

Nehemiah was hesitant to tell the king, but he blurted, "May the king live forever. Why should I not be sad when the city where my ancestors are buried lies in ruins?"

"What can I do for you?"

Nehemiah prayed a quick prayer for wisdom and then spoke, "If it please the king, send me to the city in Judah where my ancestors are buried so that I can rebuild it."

"How long will this take? When will you be back?" the king asked, and then he, the queen, and Nehemiah began working out the details of the project.

Nehemiah went to Judah and organized the local Jews to work on rebuilding the walls and reinstalling the city gate. The project was barely started when some Samaritans came by and mocked, "Look at that poor workmanship. If a fox went up it, he would break down the wall."

Despite the heckling, the Jews kept working. Seeing that teasing and mocking was not going to stop the project; the Samaritans began to intimidate them by threatening arrest. As Nehemiah and his men worked on the wall, their leader called, "What are you doing? Are you rebelling against the king? Does he know what you are doing?"

Nehemiah answered, "The Lord God will give us success; we are His servants."

Realizing the Jews had no fear of the king arresting them for rebuilding the walls; the Samaritans organized a group of thugs to beat up the workers and possibly kill them. Nehemiah, though, got word of the pending attack and posted guards.

The Samaritans then went to individual workers' homes and said, "There is so much rubble, you cannot rebuild the wall," and, as if that wasn't discouraging enough, added, "If we have to do it, we will kill you to stop the work."

"Wherever we turn, they will attack us," the discouraged workers reported to Nehemiah.

Nehemiah then assigned bodyguards to the workers and said, "Don't be afraid. The Lord is great, and He will fight for your families."

From that day on, bodyguards stood behind each person who worked, and each builder wore his sword at his side as he worked. The walls were rebuilt, the gates were rehung, and Jews who had been scattered around the world began to return to their native Jerusalem.

DEVOTIONAL THOUGHT

Don't expect everybody to be happy for you and to encourage you when you begin a new project. When you set about working on a goal, you are going to run into hecklers and bullies, just like the Jewish workers did. Just like the Jewish workers did, you are likely to get discouraged in such circumstances. For instance, you may tell your parents you want to go to college to study for a profession, and they tell you they don't have the money and you don't have the brains. Those words hurt, but if you truly want to go, you will earn the money and go. In times of discouragement, remember your goal and why you undertook it.

For Christians, this story is yet another example of how you will overcome great odds if you are doing what God has called you to do. It is also a cautionary tale that doing God's work does not mean that you will have an easy life.

For secular people, this is a story about setting and meeting one's goal. A goal should be specific and challenging but doable, something that rebuilding the walls was for Nehemiah, a high official in the king's court. A goal should have a timetable associated with it, something the king required when he asked when Nehemiah would resume his role in the palace. A goal should be worthwhile, and rebuilding the walls was.

QUESTIONS TO PONDER

- *Why doesn't God always make life easy for the people who serve Him?*

- *What goals do I have?*

- *Run each of the goals listed above through the SMARTS test as Nehemiah did. Does the goal meet the criteria of a good goal; this is, is it a Stretch, Measurable, Attainable, Relevant, Timely, and Specific?*

PRAYER

"Almighty Father, grant me confidence in You as I walk in Your will. Even if attacks come my way, I trust that through Your strength, I will be triumphant. Let no obstacle or opposition shake my faith, for I know victory is in Your hands. Amen."

PART 2

STORIES FROM
THE NEW TESTAMENT

CHAPTER 26

>>>>>>>>>>>>>>>>>>>>>>>✝<<<<<<<<<<<<<<<<<<<<<<<

MARY AND JOSEPH TRAVEL TO BETHLEHEM: EVEN GOOD PEOPLE FACE TOUGH TIMES

> " *2 Consider it pure joy, my brothers and sisters, whenever you face trials of many kinds, 3 because you know that the testing of your faith produces perseverance.*
>
> *- James 1:2-3* "

THE STORY

Rome was a vast empire, covering much of Europe, Asia, and Africa. Caesar Augustus, the Roman emperor, was curious about the resources and people in his empire, so he issued a decree that a census should be taken of the entire Roman world. The decree went on to stipulate that each male was to return to his city of origin to be counted.

Joseph was a carpenter in a small town called Nazareth in the northern part of Israel. His ancestor was King David, and so the decree required that he and his wife go to Bethlehem, David's hometown. Joseph sighed when he heard the decree. Not only was it a multi-day trip, but he would have to make it with the woman he was pledged to marry, a woman who was with child – and it wasn't his child.

Joseph had wrestled with what to do when he learned that the girl he was engaged to, Mary, was with child. He could have accused his girlfriend of adultery and had her stoned; the thought had crossed his mind, but in a dream, God had assured him that he was to raise the child as his and that the child was an immaculate conception. Joseph believed it; he doubted if the census takers would.

When the time came to travel to take the survey, Joseph saddled the donkey, put Mary on it, and headed to Jerusalem – the place many others were heading to also. Bethlehem was a small farming town, but because of the census, hundreds of people who had roots dating back to David had come into town.

As luck would have it, all the inns were full. Joseph was at a loss for what to do. Finally, one innkeeper took pity on them and offered them a stable. It wasn't a room with a bed, but there was hay there, and there was a roof over their head. Seeing Mary couldn't go much further, the soon-to-be-wed couple accepted the stable.

That night, the baby was born. Mary wrapped him in clothes and placed him in a manger. Joseph looked on lovingly and pondered what he was a part of. He suddenly realized how it had all come together – he had been told in a dream that Mary was carrying the Messiah, and he had heard the Messiah would be born in Bethlehem - and he suddenly realized the scriptures had been fulfilled.

DEVOTIONAL THOUGHT

Have you ever walked through the woods and all you could see was the trees around you? The trees were so close you could see the layers of bark, see sap oozing from a recently broken branch, and feel the texture of the leaves on your skin. When you're standing that close to a tree in the woods, you cannot see the complete forest.

Joseph had been looking at his problems – saving money for the trip, taking a long trip, dealing with a girlfriend who was carrying a child that was not his, and having to provide for mother and prospective child on the long journey. On the night Jesus was born, though, he could finally see the big picture.

It is easy to get caught up with a particular problem and not see how God is working; to believe that God is working when one can't see it at the moment requires faith. When encountering a problem, remember that all things work together for good.

QUESTIONS TO PONDER

- *What problems am I facing at the moment?*

- *Why doesn't God make life easy for the people who love him? (God loved Joseph, but he was under a lot of stress. God loved Mary, but her being pregnant made her an outcast, and having to make the trip threatened her health.)*

- *What does it mean when someone says to "live by faith"?*

PRAYER

"Almighty Father, even though I face difficulties in life despite striving to be good, I trust that these struggles are strengthening my faith and drawing me closer to You. Help me endure with patience, knowing that through faith, I move further from sin and closer to Your grace. Amen."

CHAPTER 27

>>>>>>>>>>>>>>>>>>>>>>>✝<<<<<<<<<<<<<<<<<<<<<<<

SHEPHERDS VISIT THE BABY JESUS: THE MEANING OF CONTENTMENT

> *I am not saying this because I am in need, for I have learned to be content whatever the circumstances.*
>
> *- Philippians 4:11*

THE STORY

Bethlehem was farm country, and a major commodity raised in the area was sheep. Many of these sheep were sold to the temple in Jerusalem. Jews were supposed to come to the temple at certain times of the year to make sacrifices, and many out-of-towners could not bring animals with them, so they bought unblemished animals grown locally. These shepherds in Bethlehem knew about sacrificial lambs.

On the night Jesus was born, some shepherds were in their fields watching their flocks. The night was quiet, as most nights were. Of course, a shepherd always had to be on guard for wolves and other predators. Shepherds know to expect the unexpected, but the shepherds on the outskirts of Bethlehem never anticipated what happened that night.

That night, as they were watching their flocks, an angel appeared; the angel was so holy they could barely look at him. These shepherds, who could face wolves and bears without flinching, were scared. In fact, they were terrified.

The angel sensed their fear and said, "Don't be afraid." A couple of the shepherds lifted their eyes upward, and the angel continued, "I bring you good news. Tonight, in the city of David, a Savior has been born, the Messiah, the Lord. Here is how you will recognize him; you will find him wrapped in swaddling clothes and lying in a manger."

Suddenly, the angel was joined by numerous other angels who praised God, saying, "Glory to God in the highest, and on earth, peace."

The angels disappeared as quickly as they had appeared, and the shepherds found themselves standing in the field with just their sheep. The shepherds looked at each other in disbelief, waiting for someone else to speak first. Finally, one of them said, "Let's go to Bethlehem and check out what the angel told us about."

The shepherds hurried off and found Mary and Joseph, as well as the baby, who was lying in the manger. They knelt down and worshiped him, and then they told Mary and Joseph everything the angels had said.

Once they had seen Jesus, the shepherds returned to their flocks. As they walked back to the hillside with their sheep, they told everyone they saw about the baby and what they had been told about him. Those who heard it were amazed at what the shepherds said. The shepherds were singing songs, glorifying God, and praising God for everything they had heard and seen – it was just as the angel said it would be.

DEVOTIONAL THOUGHT

What's the secret of contentment? If you chase power, there will always be someone more powerful than you. If you chase education, there will always be more to learn. If you chase riches, there will always be new models coming out. The secret to contentment – to peace – is exactly what the angel said, "Glory to God." If you have the right relationship with God, peace will follow.

Power, education, and riches are not evil, but they alone will never satisfy. A right relationship with God – and that relationship looks very different from person to person – is the only way you will have contentment. You can have power, education, and riches with a right relationship with God, and you will be content, but if you have power, education, and/or riches without God, you will feel that something is lacking in your life.

QUESTIONS TO PONDER

- *What do I prioritize as the most important in my life – obtaining money, having friends, having power, having a right relationship with God, or something else?*

- *What does it mean to be content?*

- *Why would a contented person still want to have goals for life?*

PRAYER

"Almighty Father, I thank You for the countless blessings in my life. I am grateful for the contentment in my heart, knowing that money and material things are temporary. My love, faith, and knowledge of You are what truly matter, above all else. Amen."

CHAPTER 28

>>>>>>>>>>>>>>>>>>>>>>>>>>>✝<<<<<<<<<<<<<<<<<<<<<<<<<

WISEMEN FROM THE EAST VISIT JESUS: FOLLOWING A GUIDING LIGHT

> *The light shines in the darkness, and the darkness has not overcome it.*
>
> *- John 1:5*

THE STORY

Processions of out-of-town dignitaries visiting Jerusalem were nothing new. Even though Rome currently occupied Israel, the Romans allowed the Israelites to keep most of their Israelite ways. Israel was currently under the rule of a Roman-appointed king, King Herod. King Herod found himself trying to please the Romans, the Israelites, and, most of all, himself. Seeing men riding in from Persia was not uncommon, and it was not uncommon for such men to go to the palace to pay homage to the king. What these men had to say, though, sent shockwaves through the palace, "Where is the one who has been born king of the Jews? We saw his star when it rose and have come to worship him."

Herod knew his wife had not borne a child recently, so he was deeply disturbed. Although Herod had rebuilt Solomon's temple to please his Jewish subjects, Herod had no attachment to the Jewish religion and its ban on astrology; when these wise men from the East said they had seen a star that said a king had been born, Herod believed them.

Herod knew he was living in an era when some said the Messiah would be born, and Herod feared that this was the king to which the wise men referred. He sent the wise men out of the room, called the chief priests and teachers of the law, and asked where the Messiah was to be born. Referring to the fourth chapter of Micah, the priests replied, "In Bethlehem in Judea,"

Herod thanked the priests, ushered them out, and called the Magi back into the room for a secret meeting. He inquired when the star had first appeared; it was almost two years ago. He then told them what the priests had said and sent them to Bethlehem, saying, "Go and search carefully for the child. As soon as you find him, report to me so that I, too, may go and worship him." (Herod had no intent to worship him; no threat to the throne could be allowed to exist.)

Bethlehem was about ten miles away from Jerusalem, and the wise men began to dutifully make their way there. As they walked, the star they had seen earlier rose and went ahead of them, stopping where the child was.

When they saw the star, they were overjoyed. They followed the star to a house in Bethlehem. On coming to the house, they saw the child with his mother, Mary, and they bowed down and worshiped him. As part of their worship, they opened their treasures and presented Him with gifts of gold, frankincense, and myrrh.

The Magi intended to honor their commitment to Herod, but having been warned in a dream not to go back to Herod, they returned to their country by another route.

DEVOTIONAL THOUGHT

Do you ever get to the point where you think you know what God wants for your life? The Magi may have been known for their wisdom, but even they made an assumption instead of trying to continue to seek God's will closely. The Magi had been following a star that told of the birth of a king who would rule over all nations. They had set out in search of that king, heading westward but having no idea of how far west they would be going. Eventually, they realized they were going to Israel, and it made sense to them that the king would be born in the palace in Jerusalem. They had followed the star for hundreds of miles, but in their excitement of reaching their destination, they had taken their eyes off it and had relied on "common sense."

The king had not been born in Jerusalem, however. The wise men realized they had taken their eyes off the star and had followed their own thinking. Having learned from Herod that the birth may have occurred in Bethlehem, they headed in that direction. They were overjoyed when they saw the star again, and this time, they followed it to exactly where it led.

QUESTIONS TO PONDER

- *God doesn't use stars to communicate with people today; how does God communicate with me? How do I know that I am living as God says I am to live?*

- *What are some things that can cause me to take my eyes off God?*

- *The Magi found themselves in Jerusalem instead of Bethlehem because they took their eyes off the star. Everyone gets off the path God hoped for them from time to time; when I catch myself off the path, how can I get back on?*

PRAYER

"Almighty Father, I desire to live the life You want for me, though I may not fully understand Your will. Let Your light shine upon me, guiding my steps as You led the wise men. If I stray, please make my path straight again. Amen."

CHAPTER 29

THE BAPTISM OF JESUS: PUTTING ONESELF IN THE PLACE OF OTHERS

> *inally, all of you, be like-minded, be sympathetic, love one another, be compassionate and humble.*
>
> *- 1 Peter 3:8*

THE STORY

Over four hundred years had passed since the prophet Isaiah predicted, "A voice will cry in the wilderness, 'Prepare the way of the Lord; make straight the path for him,' and excitement was in the air, for villagers now heard a voice in the woods outside town saying, "Repent, for the Kingdom of Heaven is near."

The voice belonged to John the Baptist. John even looked like the prophets of old. His clothes were made of camel hair, and he had a leather belt around his waist. His diet was locusts and wild honey. People heard him, and soon, other people came from near and far to listen to him preach, confess their sins, and be baptized in the Jordan River.

John welcomed these people, but one day, when he saw religious leaders coming, he said, "You brood of vipers. Shape up your lives. Do not think 'We have Abraham as our father' will save you from the coming wrath." John spoke the truth boldly, and some even thought he was the return of the great prophet Elijah.

To all, John declared, "I baptize you with water for repentance, but one much greater comes after me; He will baptize you with the Holy Spirit."

One day, Jesus came to be baptized by John. John initially declined, saying, "I need to be baptized by you, not you by me."

Jesus replied, "Baptize me. It is proper for us to do this to fulfill God's will."

John baptized Jesus by dunking him into the water. As Jesus came out of the water, the Spirit of God descended onto him like a dove, and a voice from heaven said, "This is my Son, whom I love; with him I am well pleased."

DEVOTIONAL THOUGHT

John the Baptist baptized people as a sign of their repentance. Jesus was sinless, and John recognized it; he, therefore, initially declined to baptize Jesus. Jesus, though, insisted that it be done. By being baptized, Jesus identified with sinners, doing something sinners would do. When he was on the cross, he took on the sins of all people. The ritual of baptism symbolized his upcoming death – His dying for the world's sin was symbolized by going under water, and the resurrection was symbolized by His coming up from the water. As He rose, a voice from Heaven said, "This is my Son; with him I am well pleased."

Jesus was not a sinner, but He could identify with sinners. He was able to "walk a mile in their shoes" and to see the world through their perspective. Because He could see through the eyes of a sinner and yet not be a sinner, He could best minister to sinners. If you want to help someone, you need to see the world from their perspective, not your perspective.

If you are going into sales, you will need to see the world from the view of a client; if you are going to be a teacher, you must see it through the eyes of a student; if you are going to be an evangelizing pastor, you must see it through the eyes of a secular person; if you are going to be a nurse, you need to see the world through the eyes of a patient. As a teen, if you want to please your parents, you need to think like an adult; if you want a top grade on an assignment, you need to think like a teacher. Ask yourself, if I were them, what would I expect – and then try to deliver it.

We all see the world from a perspective. As a teen, you see things differently than an infant does or as a senior adult does. To understand what an infant or a senior adult is thinking, you must try to see the world through their eyes. They may see the same reality that you do, but they interpret things differently.

QUESTIONS TO PONDER

- *Why is the world full of liberals and conservatives if everyone sees the same facts?*

- *How can I best relate to someone who sees the world from a different point of view than I do?*

- *If someone sees the world differently than I do, are they necessarily wrong? Can we both be right? Could we both be wrong?*

PRAYER

"Almighty Father, help me see the world from a different perspective, through the eyes of others. Teach me not to judge quickly but to understand their experiences and struggles with compassion. Guide my heart to be open, kind, and empathetic in all things. Amen."

CHAPTER 30

>>>>>>>>>>>>>>>>>>>>✝<<<<<<<<<<<<<<<<<<<<<

JESUS CALLS HIS FIRST DISCIPLES: ALWAYS BE PREPARED FOR OPPORTUNITY

> 66 *Every good and perfect gift is from above, coming down from the Father of the heavenly lights, who does not change like shifting shadows.*
>
> *- James 1:17* 99

THE STORY

The day after he baptized Jesus, John saw that Jesus was walking nearby and shouted to the crowd, "Behold, the Lamb of God, who takes away the sin of the world! This is whom I meant when I said someone was coming who is greater than me. He is the reason I am here doing what I do; I am revealing him as the Messiah. I saw the Spirit come down as a dove and remain on him; I have seen and testify that this is God's Chosen One."

When two of John's disciples heard this, they rose and followed Jesus. Jesus saw them behind him and asked, "What do you want?"

"Teacher, where are you staying?"

"Come and see," Jesus replied.

The two went with him and spent the day with him. Andrew, one of the two, was so impressed by what Jesus had to say that when evening was falling and his time with Jesus was over, he excitedly told his brother, Simon, "We have found the Messiah."

Andrew brought Simon to Jesus. Jesus looked at Simon and said, "You are Simon, son of John. You will be called Peter, which means rock."

A few days later, Jesus was walking by the seashore when he saw Peter and Andrew casting their net into the lake. (Peter and Andrew were career fishermen.) Jesus called, "Follow me, and I will send you to fish for people."

They instantly left their nets and followed him.

The three of them continued to walk down the seashore. Jesus saw two other brothers, James and John. They were in their boat with their dad, preparing their nets. Jesus called to them, and they immediately left their boat and their father to follow him.

DEVOTIONAL THOUGHT

Does opportunity scare you? It should; it can take your life in a whole new direction.

Peter and Andrew were fishermen. They were also very interested in learning about the Messiah and had followed John the Baptist. They had been exposed to the teachings of Jesus. When Jesus announced that he was starting his career ministry and invited them to follow him, they accepted instantly. (To be asked to come study under a rabbi was a great honor.)

Opportunity always involves sacrifice. The first four disciples had to leave their fishing business; James and John had to leave their father as well. Any time you decide to pursue one decision, you are closing doors to other opportunities. Are you willing to make the sacrifices required to pursue the opportunities you really want?

For Christians, this story is a reminder that Jesus is calling and that they need to answer that call. Answering will involve sacrifices, but it will be well worth those sacrifices. For the secular person, it is a reminder to prepare for what is ahead, such as Andrew did by going to where Jesus was staying, so that when opportunity calls, one knows exactly how one will respond.

QUESTIONS TO PONDER

- *The invitation to follow Jesus is extended to me, and will be there as long as I live. Am I going to take it immediately? Am I going to be like Andrew and seek to learn more? Am I going to decline it?*

- *What am I doing today to prepare for my long-term future? (For instance, if you plan to go to college, you will likely want to take college prep courses in middle school and high school.)*

- *Should I seek out opportunities or simply let opportunities come to me? Why?*

PRAYER

"Almighty Father, prepare my heart to be open to the opportunities You place before me. Like the disciples who left their catch to follow You, help me release all distractions and run to Your call with faith and readiness. Guide me in Your purpose. Amen."

CHAPTER 31

>>>>>>>>>>>>>>>>>✝<<<<<<<<<<<<<<<<

JESUS CHANGES WATER INTO WINE: SIGNS OF PROMISE

> For we are God's handiwork, created in Christ Jesus to do good works, which God prepared in advance for us to do.
>
> - Ephesians 2:10

THE STORY

One day, when Jesus was attending a wedding with his disciples, his mother approached him and said, "They have no more wine."

"Woman, why do you involve me? My hour has not yet come."

Mary didn't bother to reply; she just turned to the bridegroom's servants and said, "Do whatever he tells you."

Jesus pointed to the six stone water jars used for ceremonial washing; each could hold twenty to thirty gallons. "Fill those with water," he instructed the servants. After the servants had filled them to the brim with water, he said, "Now draw some out and take it to the master of the banquet."

The servants did as he said. The master of the banquet tasted the water, except when he tasted it, it wasn't water – it was wine.

The master of the banquet did not realize where it came from, although the servants knew. He pulled the bridegroom aside and said, "Everyone brings out choice wine first and then cheaper wine after guests have had too much to drink, but you have saved the best till now."

His disciples had seen it all. Turning water into wine was the first sign through which Jesus revealed his glory to them; his disciples saw this and believed he was who he said he was.

DEVOTIONAL THOUGHT

Jesus had shown signs of promise. His mother had confidence he could help the bridegroom who had run out of wine. His disciples had left their professions and were traipsing around with him. They saw potential, and by performing signs such as turning water into wine, he reaffirmed their confidence in him.

You have likely shown promise. Your teachers, your parents, your friends, and others have ideas about where you are going in life. You may not know all of the details yet – as Jesus said, "My time has not yet come" – but they can see potential and make predictions. They believe in you, and they want to be a part of your life.

Do you see potential in yourself? You have some.

- *What talents and skills do I have?*

- *Talents and skills provide a lot of possibilities; what are some potential options for me?*

- *Which option am I most likely to pursue? Why?*

- *What steps must I take to make that option a reality; what goals do I have?*

EXERCISE

Have someone you trust write down talents that they see in you. Compare their list to your list of your talents and skills. They may see things in you that you have not seen.

PRAYER

"Almighty Father, I thank You for the hidden talent within me, waiting to be discovered and nurtured. I promise to develop it to its full potential, knowing that this gift is from You. Guide me to use it in alignment with Your will for my life. Amen."

CHAPTER 32

>>>>>>>>>>>>>>>>>>>>>✝<<<<<<<<<<<<<<<<<<<<<

THE WOMAN AT THE WELL: WHITE LIES ARE STILL LIES

> ❝
>
> *The Lord detests lying lips,*
> *but he delights in people who are trustworthy.*
>
> *- Proverbs 12:22*
> ❞

THE STORY

As Jesus wandered the countryside preaching and healing, his travels took him into an area populated by Samaritans, people who had Jewish ancestry but also roots in other cultures. (People with two Jewish parents typically shunned these people. Rather than bypass the area, though, Jesus cut straight through it, pausing to rest at the historic well that the patriarch Jacob had dug hundreds of years before.

Jesus sent His disciples to buy food while He rested at the well. As He rested, a woman from Samaria came to draw water.

"Give me a drink," Jesus requested.

"Do you know what I am?" the woman asked. "I'm a Samaritan. Don't you realize Jews don't deal with Samaritans?"

Jesus replied, "If you know who it is who says to you, 'Give me a drink,' you would have asked him for living water, and he would have given it."

The woman chuckled. "You have nothing to draw water with,

and the well is very deep. Where do you get that living water? Are you greater than Jacob, who gave us this well?"

Jesus replied, "Whoever drinks this water will thirst again, but whoever drinks the water I give will never thirst again. The water I provide provides a fountain of everlasting life."

The woman answered, "Sir, give me this water so that I may not thirst nor come here to draw water ever again."

Jesus replied, "Go, call your husband, and come here."

The woman stated, "I have no husband."

Jesus said to her, "You say 'I have no husband,' for you have had five husbands, and the person you are with now is not your husband; you have spoken truly."

The woman replied, "Sir, I perceive you're a prophet. Tell me who is right. Our fathers worshiped on this mountain, and you Jews say that Jerusalem is where one should worship."

Jesus replied, "The hour is coming when people will worship neither here nor in Jerusalem. Instead, true worshippers will worship the Father in spirit and truth."

The woman stated, "I know the Messiah is coming. When he comes, he will tell us all things."

Jesus replied, "I who speak to you is he."

Just then, his disciples returned and marveled that He talked with a woman. No one dared to ask Him, "Why are you talking to her?"

The woman left her waterpot, went to the city, and said to the men, "Come, see a Man who told me all things I ever did. Could this be the Christ?" Upon hearing this, the men rose and came to Jesus.

Many Samaritans believed in Him because of the woman's testimony. Many others believed because they heard Him for themselves. The Samaritans urged Him to stay with them, and He stayed there for two days before resuming His travels.

DEVOTIONAL THOUGHT

What do you do when you are caught in an embarrassing situation? When Jesus told the woman to get her husband, she was caught in an embarrassing situation. She was living with someone who was not her husband. In Jesus' day, rabbis frowned upon unmarried people living together. She, therefore, told what many call a white lie; she didn't outright lie, but she omitted the truth.

White lies are considered trivial and, just like in this case, are often told because the truth would make people uncomfortable. Like the woman at the well, many people try to lie to God, glossing over the truth. God knows the truth; there is no reason to tell him lies and half-truths.

Most lies – called black lies to distinguish them from white lies – are sneaky and manipulative. Ethically, these are clearly wrong. White lies are not meant to hurt someone; they are designed to protect someone or to make someone feel good. For instance, if your four-year-old nephew asks if you like the picture of the dinosaur that he drew and you don't like it, you may lie and say that you do, even though you don't. Likewise, if your sister is proud of a new dish she made for supper, you may compliment it even though you don't care for it. These are still lies, though, and if they later find out that you did not share your true feelings, you will lose a lot of their trust.

- *Are white lies okay, especially if the truth hurts? Why or why not?*

- *If my friend asks if I like her new haircut, and I don't like it, should I lie and say that it looks great? Why or why not?*

- *Is it okay to lie to children? For instance, some parents tell their children to stay in bed so the creature under the bed won't grab their legs in the night.*

- *Many people consider the terms "white lies" and "black lies" to lead to racial prejudice; that is, white is good, and black is bad. What terms can I use instead?*

PRAYER

"Almighty Father, help me to be an honest and trustworthy person, avoiding the sin of lying. Keep me from misleading others, even with white lies, and guide my words to speak truth. Though I may not mean harm, I ask for Your wisdom to speak with integrity. Amen."

CHAPTER 33

KING HEROD EXECUTES JOHN THE BAPTIST: BE CAREFUL OF THE PROMISES YOU MAKE

> *When a man makes a vow to the Lord or takes an oath to obligate himself by a pledge, he must not break his word but must do everything he said.*
>
> *- Numbers 30:2*

THE STORY

When King Herod the Great died, the Romans divided Israel into three sections and gave a third to each of his sons to rule. Herod

– he was officially Herod, Jr. - inherited the third that included Galilee where John the Baptist baptized. When John the Baptist started calling Herod and the queen out for adultery - Herod had married his brother Philip's ex-wife - the queen, Herodias, insisted that Herod arrest John and kill him.

To get the nagging to stop, Herod did arrest John, but he had him placed in prison, not killed. Herod knew John was a righteous person; he feared him, and he kept him safe. Herod even enjoyed listening to John, although what John said made little sense to him.

Herodias continued to pester him about killing John, but Herod would not do it. One night, though, she found the opportunity. When Herod held a banquet on his birthday and invited all the nobles, military commanders, and leading men of Galilee to celebrate the occasion with him, her daughter, Salome, danced as entertainment. Herod and the guests were so wowed by her. Herod said, "Ask me anything you wish, up to half my kingdom, and I will give it to you."

Salome had no idea of what to ask, so she went to her mother and said, "For what should I ask?"

"The head of John the Baptist," Herodias replied.

Salome returned to the party and, in front of the guests, said to the king, "I want the head of John the Baptist on a platter."

Herod was saddened at the request, but he had made an oath in front of everyone and did not want to break his word. He immediately gave an executioner the order to bring John's head to him.

The executioner then went to the prison, beheaded John, put the head on a platter, and then handed the platter to Salome, who then gave it to her mother.

Be careful what you promise people. Herod made a promise in front of very important people, and when he realized he had not acted wisely, he still went through with the oath to save face in front of his guests. A person's word carried a lot of weight in those days, and breaking it would have ruined his reputation; today, too, if you say you are going to do something, you need to do it, or people will no longer trust you.

Jesus advised his followers, "Do not take an oath at all." In many cases, there are unseen consequences when one takes an oath. Herod certainly did not intend to take the life of John the Baptist, but that was an unexpected consequence. Herod did not intend to stop pondering religion, but with John out of his life, he focused on affairs of the state and parties, giving little thought to religion.

Oaths, especially those made rashly, should be avoided. There are times, though, when oath-making is expected, and these carefully thought-out oaths are intended to serve as guiding principles. Doctors take an oath to do no harm; I want my doctor to honor that. In court, people swear to tell the truth, the whole truth; if the truth is to be discovered and the pieces put together, people need to be honest. When immigrants become citizens, they swear an oath to their new country; their old country may call upon them, but those around them need to be assured they are going to be loyal to their new nation. By following these oaths, people know what to do even if they are tempted to do something else.

- *Swearing "by God" to do something and then not doing it is considered blasphemy, breaking the first of the Ten Commandments. If I swear something "by God", should I go ahead and do it, especially if I later find it was a foolish oath?*

- *Have I made any oaths?*

- *Instead of swearing an oath, what can I do to show people that I am serious about what I am saying?*

PRAYER

"Almighty Father, help me to be careful in making promises. Grant me the wisdom to commit only to what I can fulfill and to avoid making foolish promises that could harm others. Guide my words so that I always uphold my commitments with integrity. Amen."

CHAPTER 34

>>>>>>>>>>>>>>>>>>>✝<<<<<<<<<<<<<<<<<<

JESUS FEEDS THE CROWD OF 5,000 MEN: GIVING ALL ONE HAS, NO MATTER HOW LITTLE, MAKES A DIFFERENCE

> ❝ *Give generously to them and do so without a grudging heart; then because of this the Lord your God will bless you in all your work and in everything you put your hand to.*
>
> *- Deuteronomy 15:10* ❞

THE STORY

Curious about what Jesus would do next, many people followed Jesus from the town where he had healed the sick to the shore of the Sea of Galilee. As they started up a hill, Jesus and his disciples could see the large crowd trailing them. Seeing the crowd coming toward them, Jesus turned to his disciple Philip and asked, "Where are we going to buy food for all of these folks?"

Philip replied, "Even if there was a store around here, we don't have the funds. It would take half a year of wages to buy each person just one bite."

Andrew saw a boy who had brought his own lunch, so he motioned for the boy to come over to them. The boy nervously approached, and Andrew said, "Here is a boy with five small barely loaves and two small fish. I don't think they'll go very far."

"May I?" Jesus asked the little boy, motioning for the basket of food. As the boy willingly gave it to him, Jesus told Philip and Andrew, "Have the people sit down."

Once everyone was seated – there were about 5,000 men, as well as women and children, Jesus held up the basket of bread, gave a blessing, and let everyone eat as much as they wanted. He then held up the basket of fish, gave a blessing, and let everyone eat as much of it as they wanted to as well.

When everyone was full, Jesus said to his disciples, "Gather the leftovers; let nothing be wasted." The disciples willingly gathered the food, filling twelve baskets full of bread. As the disciples collected the bread, people remembered there were only five loaves to begin with, and they realized they had witnessed a miracle. "Surely this is the Messiah," they began to say in amazement. As the conversation continued, Jesus could sense that they were murmuring about anointing him king, so he quietly slipped away.

DEVOTIONAL THOUGHT

Do you feel like you have nothing to offer to God or the world? Although there will always be someone who is smarter than you, richer than you, more experienced than you, or more skilled than you, that does not mean that you should not try to make a difference. Just as Jesus was able to feed a crowd of over 10,000 – 5,000 men and likely as many women and children - with five barley loaves and two fish, your contribution can be used to do great things.

For instance, you may not think that giving a mere dollar to a worthwhile cause makes any difference, but if 100 people would do it, the cause would have $100! You may not be able to go to a protest rally, but perhaps you could make a sign for a protester to carry. You may not be able to help every elderly person but if you simply look after the one who lives near you, you are making a big difference.

It's easy to come up with excuses not to make a difference. "I'm too young," "I'm not living in the right place," and "I'm too busy" are common excuses. No excuse is a good excuse; we can all make a difference.

QUESTIONS TO PONDER

- *What are some things I can do to enhance the life of someone or to better my neighborhood?*

- *It's tempting to see oneself as insignificant and to believe that one can't do anything, but one CAN do something. What are some things that I could do?*

- *Having realized that there are things I can do, here comes the tough question: What will I do? For many, coming up with things that could be done is easy, but to actually do them is not. What will I do?*

PRAYER

"Almighty Father, I desire to make a difference in this world, whether through small acts or great ones. Help me to live in a way that enhances Your glory and impacts the lives of others and myself for good. Guide my actions to reflect Your love. Amen."

CHAPTER 35

PETER WALKS ON WATER: KEEP YOUR EYES ON WHAT'S IMPORTANT – NOT ON THE CRAZINESS AROUND YOU

> *Trust in the Lord with all your heart*
> *and lean not on your own understanding;*
>
> *- Proverbs 3:5*

Jesus and his disciples often traveled from place to place by boat. One day, having finished preaching to a crowd and providing supper to them, Jesus asked his disciples to take the boat to their next location while he went up a mountainside to pray.

When the disciples were quite a distance from land, a violent storm came up. The wind and the waves blew the boat off course. From his mountain view, Jesus could see the disciples battling the waves, trying to get the boat back on course. With the storm still raging, at dawn, Jesus started toward them – walking on the lake!

The disciples saw him approaching through the storm and were terrified. "It's a ghost!" someone cried, pointing to Jesus in horror.

"It's just me," Jesus soothed, continuing to walk toward them. "Don't be afraid."

"He's walking on water," someone else gasped.

"Lord, if that's really you, let me come walk with you," said Peter.

"Come," Jesus invited, offering an outstretched hand.

Peter sat on the edge of the boat, put his feet in the water, and then started to walk toward Jesus as the storm raged around him. He was almost to where Jesus was when he became conscious of what he was doing. Instead of looking at Jesus, he looked at the waves, and he became afraid – and he started to sink. "Lord, save me!" he called as he bobbed in the thrashing water.

Jesus immediately put his hand out and pulled Peter up to him. Hugging him, he reprimanded, "You of little faith, why did you doubt?"

Hand in hand, they walked on the water as the waves billowed around them and the wind blew mist in their faces. Jesus helped Peter into the boat and then got in himself. As soon as they were in the boat, the storm ceased. The disciples marveled, "Truly, you are the Son of God."

Life is full of storms. Bad things happen to good people. Relationships go sour. Misfortune strikes. Like it or not, storms rage all around us.

In the midst of these storms, it is important to remember what is truly important. From a Christian viewpoint, nothing is more important than God. By keeping one's eyes focused on God, one can get through the tough time. From a secular standpoint, the most important thing might be a goal, such as graduating. In the case of graduating, focusing on the big goal helps us avoid dwelling on the little setbacks and the hard work that is required.

Not everything that is "urgent" is important. Taking care of the boat was an urgent concern for Peter, but being with Jesus was far more important. For us, watching the sporting event live may be urgent – the opportunity will come and go – but it may not be as important as studying is. Not everything urgent is important, and to succeed in life, one must focus on the important matters.

QUESTIONS TO PONDER

- *What storms in my life am I currently facing? What methods am I using to cope with them?*

- *What do I focus on in life? What is more important than anything else?*

- *Why is it so easy to get distracted from what is most important? How can I better ensure that I stay focused?*

- *What is the difference between an "urgent task" and an "important task"? What is an example of each?*

PRAYER

"Almighty Father, with so much happening in this world, help me to focus on what truly matters. Guide me to choose what aligns with Your will and place all my attention on it. If You are at the center, I know it is what's important. Amen."

CHAPTER 36

>>>>>>>>>>>>>>>>>>>>> ✝ <<<<<<<<<<<<<<<<<<<<<

THE TRANSFIGURATION OF JESUS: MOVING ON FROM LIFE'S HIGH POINTS

> *16 For we did not follow cleverly devised stories when we told you about the coming of our Lord Jesus Christ in power, but we were eyewitnesses of his majesty. 17 He received honor and glory from God the Father when the voice came to him from the Majestic Glory, saying, "This is my Son, whom I love; with him I am well pleased."*
>
> *- 2 Peter 1:16-17*

THE STORY

One day, Peter, James, and John had hiked up a mountainside with Jesus while the other disciples stayed below. Jesus often went off alone to pray, possibly taking one or two disciples to pray with him or to teach. On this day, though, something totally unexpected happened. When they got to the mountaintop, Jesus was transfigured before them. His face was as bright as the sun; his clothes became whiter than light. As if this wasn't amazing enough, suddenly, the disciples saw Moses and Elijah talking with Jesus.

Upon seeing the three together, Peter spoke up, saying, "Lord, it's good we are here. If you'd like, I'll put up three shelters – one for you, one for Moses, and one for Elijah."

Peter was still talking when a bright cloud covered them; a voice from within the cloud said, "This is my Son, whom I love; with him I am well pleased. Listen to him."

Upon hearing this, the disciples fell facedown, terrified. Jesus came and touched them, saying, "Get up. Don't be afraid."

When the disciples looked up, they saw no one except Jesus.

Jesus then led them down the mountain to where the other disciples were waiting. As they walked, He instructed, "Don't tell anyone what you have seen until the Son of Man has risen from the dead."

DEVOTIONAL THOUGHT

The disciples had a literal mountaintop experience. They were on an emotional high. They had seen Jesus transfigured; they had seen Moses and Elijah; they had heard the voice of God. Peter wanted the experience to last; he wanted to make shelters. Don't you wish mountain top experiences would last forever?

Jesus, though, led the disciples back down the mountain. They had to go back to the humdrum of daily life. Jesus, though, alluded to another mountaintop experience that was coming: His Resurrection. If they stayed forever on the mountain where they were, they could not experience an even greater event.

We, too, get very satisfied with the status quo. I always hate to see the school year come to an end; just when I've got the hang of a particular grade, I am asked to leave it. It is only by moving on, though, that I can experience greater things.

Change is a part of life. Although it is tempting to cling to the mountain top experiences, if we are to reach even greater mountain tops, we must walk through the valleys and hard times. We must climb new mountains, and some of those mountains are not easy to climb. For a Christian, there is ultimately the mountain top – one will eventually reach Heaven if one continues one's journey through life. For the secular person, the mountain tops are in the present world. In both cases, one must walk through a lot of valleys, enjoy a mountaintop experience here and there, and then journey back into the valley while heading to the next mountain.

QUESTIONS TO PONDER

- *Why didn't Jesus want the disciples to talk about the transfiguration until after His resurrection? Why is it hard to keep mountaintop experiences a secret?*

- *What are some mountaintop experiences that I have had?*

- *What was it like returning to daily life after the mountaintop experience?*

- *What are some mountaintop experiences I can expect in my future? What are some valleys that I will have to go through to get to each one of those mountaintop experiences?*

PRAYER

"Almighty Father, I know my path is filled with peaks and valleys, and while I'd rather stay on the mountaintop, I understand that I cannot fully know You there alone. Help me embrace the valleys and see Your glory, even in the lows. Amen."

CHAPTER 37

THE PARABLE OF THE SOWER: GET THE MESSAGE OUT

 *For you have been born again, not of perishable seed, but of imperishable, through the living and enduring word of God.*

- 1 Peter 1:23

THE STORY

Jesus often taught in parables, simple stories used to express moral and/or spiritual truths. One day, he told the crowd the following parable, "A farmer sowed his seed. Some seed fell along the path; it was trampled and eaten by birds. Some seed fell on rocky ground, and when they came up, the plants had no moisture and withered. Some seed fell among thorns; the thorns grew up with the plant and choked it. Some seed, though, fell on good soil; it grew and yielded a crop a hundred times what was sown."

When the crowd had gone, one of the disciples asked Jesus what the parable meant. Jesus explained, "The seeds represent God's word. The seeds that fell on the path represent those who hear but never grow the word in their heart. The seeds on the rock ground represent people who are filled with joy at first, but the gospel does not take root in their hearts. The seeds that fell among thorns represent those who hear but whose faith is choked by life's worries or life's riches and pleasures. The seeds on good soil represent those who hear the word and persevere."

DEVOTIONAL THOUGHT

In the Parable of the Sower, Jesus explains that not everyone who hears the gospel becomes a Christian. By reading this book, seeds have been sown. Some readers will not believe, some will seek to learn more, but the seed won't take root, and some will become Christians.

Jesus was focused on those who heard the gospel, but the principle he shared applies to secular issues as well. You may have a passion for the environment. You can share your views about the environment, and, just like what happens with the gospel, some won't believe, some will want to learn more but won't stick with it, and some will become an even greater advocate than you are.

Whatever issue you feel passionate about, don't expect everyone to share your enthusiasm. Like a farmer, though, keep sowing the seeds; some will take root, and you will make a difference in society!

QUESTIONS TO PONDER

- *Now that I have been exposed to the gospel, what am I going to do? Will I seek to learn more? Am I convinced Jesus is who he says, or do I think it's a bunch of bunk?*

- *What issue(s) am I passionate about?*

- *How am I going to deal with people who do not agree with me? For instance, if I oppose racism, what am I going to do when I encounter a racist?*

PRAYER

"Almighty Father, give me the strength and wisdom to face opposition when standing firm in my belief in You. Help me to boldly spread Your message, even when others think I'm out of my mind. Let Your truth guide me and give me courage. Amen."

CHAPTER 38

>>>>>>>>>>>>>>>>>>>>>>>>>>>> ✝ <<<<<<<<<<<<<<<<<<<<<<<<<<<<

THE PARABLE OF THE GOOD SAMARITAN: BEING A GOOD NEIGHBOR

> " *Do not seek revenge or bear a grudge against anyone among your people, but love your neighbor as yourself. I am the Lord.*
>
> *- Leviticus 19:18* "

THE STORY

Religious leaders were constantly trying to trip up Jesus. For instance, one day, a religious leader said to Jesus, "The scriptures state, 'Love the Lord your God with all your heart and with all your soul, and with all your strength, and with all your mind,' and 'Love your neighbor as yourself.'

Jesus nodded, "Do this."

"And who is my neighbor?"

Jesus told the following story in reply, "A Jewish man was traveling from Jerusalem to Jericho when he was attacked by robbers who stripped him, beat him, and left him half dead. A priest was going down the same road, and when he saw the man, he passed to the other side. A Levite, too, passed by on the other side. However, when a Samaritan saw him, he took pity on him. He bandaged his wounds and then put the man on his own donkey. He took the man to an inn, paid for a night, and said to the innkeeper, 'Look after him. When I return, I will reimburse you for any extra expenses you may have.' Now, sir, I ask you, which of the three do you think was a neighbor to the man who was robbed?"

The religious leader replied, "The one who had mercy on him."

Jesus told him, "Go and do likewise."

DEVOTIONAL THOUGHT

In the Parable of the Good Samaritan, a foolish man started a journey. He was foolish because it was known that robbers were hidden on the route, and therefore, one ought to caravan with friends. The man, though, went off by himself, thinking nothing bad would happen. But something bad did happen.

The foolish man was not the only one on the trail that day walking by himself. A priest and a Levite were by themselves as well. These were well-respected people in Israel - and certainly respected by the religious leader baiting Jesus - but they kept moving. To the prejudiced Jew, there was nothing worse than a Samaritan – notice the religious leader could have said, "The Samaritan" when answering Jesus but could not admit that a Samaritan could be better than a priest or a Levite, and so he instead said, "The one who had mercy on him." For Christians, this is a parable about being kind to everyone you see and not assuming societal stereotypes are correct.

As a teenager, you are going to embark on a lot of adventures – and a few of them will be foolish journeys. Although care and preparation should be taken before starting any adventure, mistakes will be made. Hopefully, muggers don't find you, but it's almost certain unexpected problems will. You will need to turn to help. Don't be surprised if some of the people you think will help don't, and likewise, don't be surprised if your help comes from an unexpected source.

Just as you will be in the role of the traveler, you will also be in the role of the Samaritan. As you travel through life, you will have the chance to help other people. Some of these people can repay you; some cannot. Will you take the time to help?

QUESTIONS TO PONDER

- *Sometimes, parables can have two meanings. This one certainly has the meaning that anyone can be anyone's neighbor. To see the second meaning, pretend the foolish traveler represents sinners and the Good Samaritan represents Jesus. When read this way, what does the parable mean?*

- *What logic did the priest and Levite use for not taking time to help? Is there ever a good reason not to help? If so, list some.*

- *If I saw somebody truly in need of help, would I make sure that they got the help they needed? Why or why not?*

PRAYER

"Almighty Father, help me love my neighbors, no matter their race, gender, or religion. Teach me to cross boundaries in kindness, offering help to those in need, just as the Good Samaritan did. Let my actions reflect Your love and compassion always. Amen."

CHAPTER 39

THE PARABLE OF THE PRODIGAL SON: NOT EVERYONE'S GOING TO BE HAPPY FOR YOU

> *No temptation has overtaken you except what is common to mankind. And God is faithful; he will not let you be tempted beyond what you can bear. But when you are tempted, he will also provide a way out so that you can endure it.*
>
> *- 1 Corinthians 10:13*

Here is another of the parables Jesus told: Once upon a time, a man had two sons. The youngest one said, "Father, give me my share of the property," so the father did. The son then went to a foreign land, where he wasted his inheritance. Completely broke, he finally found work at a pig farm feeding hogs. He was so hungry he looked longingly at the pods the hogs were eating; no one gave him anything.

When he came to himself, he said, "My father's hired servants have enough to eat. I will go to him and say, 'Father, I have sinned against you. I am no longer worthy to be called your son. Treat me as a hired servant." He then left the pig farm and headed home.

While he was a long way off, his father saw him. He ran out to meet him; he then embraced and kissed him.

His son launched into the prepared speech, saying, "Father, I have sinned; I am no longer worthy to be called your son."

His father ignored his speech, turned to a servant, and said, "Bring the best robe and put it on him; give him a ring for his hand and shoes for his feet. Kill the fatted calf! Let's eat and celebrate. My son was dead and is alive again; he was lost and is found."

The servants joined in the father's celebration. When the older son returned from the day's work in the field and heard the music and dancing coming from the house, he asked one of the servants what it meant. The servant replied excitedly, "Your brother has returned. Your father has killed the fatted calf because he made it back safely."

The servant invited him to join in the revelry, but he declined. After a while, his father came out and invited him as well. The older boy declined. When asked why, he stated, "Look, I served you for many years, and I never disobeyed you, yet you have never even given me a young goat. But when this son of yours came, this son who devoured your property with sinful living, you killed the fatted calf."

With fatherly wisdom, the old man said, "You are always with me, and all I have is yours. It is fitting to be happy, though, for your brother was dead and is alive; he was lost and is found."

DEVOTIONAL THOUGHT

The prodigal son received a great amount of blessing, but he wasted it all. When he no longer had any money, his so-called friends left him. He finally found a job working with pigs, a disgusting job for Jews of that day because pigs were considered unclean animals. The boy eventually realized he did not have to stay in these terrible circumstances. He realized his dad loved him unconditionally, and even though he had misused what was given to him, he believed he would be accepted.

He misjudged his father. His father didn't just accept him; he accepted him as a son with all the privileges that come with being a son – the ring with the family seal, clothing fit for special children, and sandals. The boy expected to be accepted somewhat begrudgingly, but his father welcomed him enthusiastically, running down the road to meet him. His father had been hoping he would turn his life around. Unfortunately, he also misjudged his brother. His brother was jealous.

From a Christian perspective, the story says that God loves us but that not every church member will be as accepting. They may remember you from your younger days and not treat you as a church member equal to themselves.

From a secular perspective, the story states that not everyone is going to be glad when you get your life straightened out. If you have clowned around with grades and start to take classes seriously, those who clowned around are going to mock you, and many of the "brains" are not going to welcome you into their clique. Doing the right thing may not make you popular with everyone, but it is still the right thing to do, and many people will celebrate the decision with you.

QUESTIONS TO PONDER

- *Jesus stopped the story with the father and oldest son talking. Do I think the older son went to the party? Why or why not?*

- *Why was the father so happy? Why was the older brother so mad? Were either right in their emotions?*

- *We all make bad choices and often follow the bad choice with another bad choice, just as the Prodigal Son did. What do I plan to do to recover next time I make a bad choice?*

PRAYER

"Almighty Father, I often find myself making the wrong choices, even when I know what's right. Please guide my heart and mind to choose wisely before I find myself in regret, like the prodigal son in the pig pen. Help me walk in Your wisdom. Amen."

CHAPTER 40

>>>>>>>>>>>>>>>>>>>>✝<<<<<<<<<<<<<<<<<<<

THE TRIUMPHAL ENTRY: IT'S OKAY TO SUBMIT TO A HIGHER POWER

> *6 Humble yourselves, therefore, under God's mighty hand, that he may lift you up in due time. 7 Cast all your anxiety on him because he cares for you.*
>
> *- 1 Peter 5:6-7*

THE STORY

Jesus and his disciples had been walking from Galilee to Jerusalem for days, teaching, preaching, and healing as they went. When they were within about ten miles of Jerusalem, Jesus asked two of his disciples, "Go to the village up ahead, and as you enter it, you will find a colt, a young donkey tied there, one that has never been ridden. Untie it and bring it here. Should anyone ask why you are untying it, reply, 'The Lord needs it.'"

The disciples walked to the village and found the colt just as He had said. As they were untying it, the owner asked, "Why are you untying the colt?"

"The Lord needs it," they replied, and the owner let them finish untying it and then take it. They brought it to Jesus, threw their cloaks on it, and put Jesus on it.

As they journeyed down the road, people came out from the village and put their cloaks or branches from palm trees on the road. Recalling the miracles they had seen, the crowd began to sing, "Blessed is the king who comes in the name of the Lord," and to shout, "Hosanna! Hosanna in the highest!"

Some of the Pharisees, religious leaders who were not ordained priests, were in the crowd and called to Jesus, "Teacher, rebuke your disciples."

Jesus replied, "If they were to keep quiet, the rocks and stones themselves would start to sing."

The procession marched to Jerusalem. When they stood on a hill overlooking the city, Jesus lamented, "Oh, Jerusalem," and cried, knowing the beautiful city would never accept Him despite His upcoming efforts to win it over. He then proceeded down the hill and into the city.

DEVOTIONAL THOUGHT

If you have grown up on a farm, you know that donkeys, horses, and other animals do not initially like to be ridden. The man who could control storms could control wild beasts as well, so it should come as no surprise to hear that Jesus rode the donkey for over ten miles that day. Not only did he ride the donkey, but he also rode the donkey without incident; donkeys are notorious for being stubborn and coming to unexpected halts.

Donkeys aren't the only things that don't like to be controlled by others. We humans don't like it either. Jesus cried because the religious establishment in Jerusalem would never accept him as their King and bow down to Him. From a Christian perspective, one must submit their will to the will of Jesus just as the donkey did; they must do what He wants.

From a secular viewpoint, the same is true – you are going to have to submit yourself to another power. If you are going to be successful, you need to submit yourself to your teacher, your spouse, and later to your boss. If you respect them, you will gladly go where they lead you and do what they tell you.

Surrendering oneself to a higher power is not always a sign of weakness. When the higher power is worthy of submitting to, one is actually growing; one is bettering oneself by following their guidance.

QUESTIONS TO PONDER

- *Why is it so hard for humans to let someone else be in charge of them?*

- *When are appropriate times to submit oneself to another person? When would be some inappropriate times?*

- *What can be gained by submitting oneself to someone else?*

PRAYER

"Almighty Father, I struggle to fully submit to Your higher power, fearing the loss of control. Yet, I know that I was never truly in control—only under the illusion of it. Help me release this illusion and surrender completely, trusting You to guide my life. Amen."

CHAPTER 41

JESUS AND THE MONEY CHANGERS: IT'S OKAY TO GET ANGRY

> *26 "In your anger do not sin": Do not let the sun go down while you are still angry, 27 and do not give the devil a foothold.*
>
> *- Ephesians 4:26-27*

THE STORY

With people waving palm branches and singing, "Blessed is he who comes in the name of the Lord," Jesus worked his way down the hill and into Jerusalem. Once inside the city gates, he headed for the temple. When he got to the temple, he stopped and got off the donkey.

What he saw at the temple appalled him. Money changers were seated next to those who sold pigeons, cattle, and oxen for sacrifices to God. (Money changers were present because Jews lived in many foreign countries, they did not have Jewish money, and Jewish money was required to buy the sacrificial animals. The money changers would give travelers Jewish coins in exchange for the foreign currency, but it was at a much higher cost than what the coins normally traded for. Meanwhile, the prices of the animals were also inflated, for the ranchers knew that the travelers could not bring their own animals from distant lands.)

Jesus walked into the temple and began overturning the tables of the money changers, dumping the coin jars, and tossing aside the seats of those who sold livestock. He made a whip from cords and drove out the money changers, ranchers, and animals, declaring, "My temple should be a house of prayer, but you have made it a den of thieves!"

The priests stood by, seething with anger, but they did not try to stop Him. By the time He had cleared out the temples, it was late afternoon; since it was getting later, He set out with His disciples for the nearby town in which He was staying.

DEVOTIONAL THOUGHT

Many people picture Jesus as mild, someone who would always turn the other cheek. Those people have the wrong picture of Jesus. Jesus knew anger, and he released it in appropriate ways. Jesus was upset that the temple system had become corrupted – not only were the money changers and the ranchers gouging the religious pilgrims for sacrificial animals, but the priests were accepting money to allow it to take place.

It is okay to get angry. There is a lot of injustice in the world. You have a right to get angry. Even Jesus got angry. However, there is a right way and a wrong way to express that anger. Jesus didn't cuss; he didn't punch anyone. Jesus simply fixed the problem and explained why he was fixing it.

You're going to have lots of reasons to get angry as you go through life. Use that anger, though, to make a positive difference.

QUESTIONS TO PONDER

- *Seeing people take something that was supposed to be holy and use it for personal gain got Jesus angry. What gets me upset?*

- *What are some alternatives to cussing and punching that I can do when I am angry?*

- *Is it okay to get angry? Why or why not?*

PRAYER

"Almighty Father, I know that anger is a natural part of being human, as we are made in Your image. Yet, I seek to control my temper and not sin in my anger. Help me resist fleshly thoughts of revenge and respond with grace and wisdom. Amen."

CHAPTER 42

>>>>>>>>>>>>>>>>>>>>✝<<<<<<<<<<<<<<<<<<<<

THE LAST SUPPER: TRUE LEADERS ARE SERVANTS

Sitting down, Jesus called the Twelve and said, "Anyone who wants to be first must be the very last, and the servant of all."

- Mark 9:35

THE STORY

>>>>>—————————————————<<<<<

One afternoon, the mother of James and John, two of Jesus's disciples, came up to Jesus and asked if He'd grant her a favor. Jesus inquired what it was. She asked that her sons be granted the privilege of sitting next to Him, one on the left and one on the right, in His kingdom. Jesus replied that those places were being assigned by the Father, not by him. When the other disciples heard what had happened, they were indignant with James and John.

That inner turmoil carried over to the Last Supper. Jesus found the Upper Room to host the supper, but they had no servant available to wash their feet, and none of the disciples were going to humble themselves to a servant's status and wash the others' feet. Finally, as the disciples ate the Passover meal, Jesus rose from the table, took off his outer garment, and wrapped a towel around his waist. He then poured water into a basin and began to wash and dry his disciples' feet, including those of Judas, the man who he knew was going to betray him.

"Lord, are you going to wash my feet?" Peter exclaimed as Jesus approached him.

"What I do, you do not understand, but you will understand later."

"You shall never wash my feet!" Peter declared.

"If I don't wash you, you can have no part with me."

"Then wash not only my feet but my hands and head, too!"

"He who has bathed needs only to wash his feet, and he is clean all over. And you are clean – though not all of you," Jesus said, acknowledging to Judas he knew what Judas planned.

Peter eventually begrudgingly let Jesus wash his feet, and Jesus moved on to the next disciple. Having washed all of their feet, he put his clothes back on and returned to his place at the table. "Do you know what I have done? You call me 'teacher' and 'Lord', for so I am. Now, if I, the Lord, have washed your feet, you should wash one another's feet as well. I have given you an example. No servant is greater than his master; no messenger is greater than the one who sent him. Do as I have done, and you will be blessed."

DEVOTIONAL THOUGHT

You've likely heard of a "right-hand man" before. The person who sat on the right-hand side of the leader was the second most powerful person in the room; the person who sat on the left-hand side was the third most important person. Even today, those who are closely aligned with the leader are the ones in the boardroom who are usually physically closest to the leader.

Jesus had lots of followers, but he had an inner circle of twelve. Those in the inner circle were jockeying for position. They wanted power in order to boss each other around. Jesus, though, taught that power wasn't to hold it over other people for one's glory; it was to minister to other people.

- *When I am in a leadership position, what kind of leader am I? Do I work for the good of the group or the good of myself? Am I willing to work side-by-side with others on yucky tasks, or do I prefer to let those of less status do them? Do I care about my teammates? Do I care about the task at hand?*

- *What are the advantages of being a servant-leader, as Jesus proposed?*

- *What are the disadvantages of the servant-leader style?*

PRAYER

"Almighty Father, the world sees leadership as a pyramid, but in Your kingdom, it's an inverted one. You lead by serving from the bottom, lifting others up. Help me follow Your example, providing what is lacking to those I lead, so they may succeed. Amen."

CHAPTER 43

JESUS ON TRIAL BEFORE PILATE: STANDING FOR TRUTH EVEN WHEN IT IS NOT POPULAR

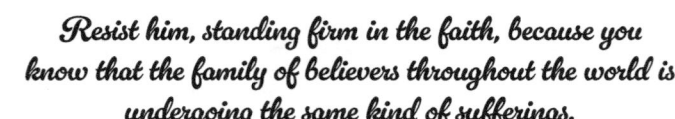

Resist him, standing firm in the faith, because you know that the family of believers throughout the world is undergoing the same kind of sufferings.

- 1 Peter 5:9

Having arrested Jesus and verified that He had proclaimed himself the Son of God – an act of blasphemy that was worthy of death from their perspective – the Jewish leaders took Jesus to the front yard of the Roman governor, Pilate, to have Pilate execute Jesus. (To show that Israel was under Roman rule, even though it had much self-rule, the Romans had taken away the Jews' ability to execute people. Knowing that Pilate was a Roman who believed that one god was as good as another god and, therefore, Pilate would not execute someone for blasphemy, when Pilate asked, "What charges do you bring against this man?" the Jews refused to say that the crime was blasphemy; instead, they retorted with a vague, "If he were not a criminal, we would not have handed him over to you to execute."

Pilate wanted nothing to do with judging Jesus. "Judge him by your own law," he said.

"We have no right to execute anyone," they objected.

Pilate sighed and invited Jesus into his palace. "Are you the king of the Jews?" he asked.

"My kingdom is not of this world."

"You are a king then!"

You say that I am. I came into the world to testify to the truth."

"What is truth?" Pilate retorted, believing everyone had their own ideas of truth. He then stepped to the door and announced, "I find no charge against him. I traditionally release a prisoner at Passover. Let me release him to you."

"No. Give us Barabbas," the leaders declared and encouraged the gathering crowd to chant with them.

Scared of an insurrection taking place if he let Jesus go, Pilate decided to try to create sympathy for Jesus. Pilate ordered Jesus to be flogged. The soldiers twisted a crown from thorns and placed it on Jesus's head. After the whipping, they put a purple robe on Jesus, said, "Hail, king of the Jews", and slapped him in the face.

Pilate opened the door again and showed the Jews the beaten Jesus wearing the crown of thorns and purple robe. "Here is the man.," he said.

"Crucify him," the chief priests said.

"He is innocent," Pilate insisted.

"We have a law, and he must die, for he has claimed to be the Son of God."

As chants of "Crucify him" increased, Pilate closed the door and said to Jesus, "Where do you come from?"

Jesus didn't answer.

"Do you realize I have the power to free you or crucify you?" Pilate asked.

"You'd have no power over me if I didn't give it to you."

Herod was in town for the Passover, so Pilate sent Jesus to Herod since Herod was the official governor of Jesus's hometown. Herod, who had put John the Baptist to death and almost lost his kingdom for doing so, declined to execute Jesus, returning him to Pilate under the pretenses of showing his respect for Rome.

Pilate kept trying to set Jesus free, but the Jewish leaders kept shouting, "Crucify him."

"Shall I crucify your king?" Pilate asked."

"We have no king but Caesar," the chief priests insisted. "If you let him go, you are no friend of Caesar's."

Perceiving he had no choice but to execute Jesus, Pilate took a basin and said, "I wash my hands of his blood. He is innocent."

"His blood be upon us," the crowd retorted.

Pilate released Barabbas and asked the Roman soldiers to crucify Jesus on the cross originally intended for Barrabas. The soldiers led Jesus, who carried his own cross much of the way, to The Place of The Skull, where they crucified him with a criminal on each side of him.

Pilate made notices to make it clear why criminals were being crucified. Pilate had a notice of "Jesus of Nazareth, the King of the Jews" placed on Jesus's cross. The sign was written in Aramaic, Latin, and Greek, thereby giving his testimony to many of the people watching. The priests protested to Pilate, saying, "Do not write 'The King of the Jews' but that he claimed to be the king of the Jews."

Pilate finally found the nerve to stand up to the priests and answered, "What I have written, I have written."

DEVOTIONAL THOUGHT

Do you want to be popular? Most people do. Do you want to do the right thing? Most people do. Much of the time, being popular and doing the right thing are the same thing, but in other cases, you can't be popular and also do the right thing.

Pilate knew Jesus was innocent of any crime. Pilate wanted to be popular, though. He had the power to simply let Jesus go, but he didn't want to upset people. Therefore, he tried to have people reach the same conclusion he had reached – Jesus had done nothing wrong. He tried a variety of methods - he encouraged Jesus to speak up; he bluntly announced his opinion that Jesus was innocent; he created sympathy by having Jesus whipped; he sent Jesus to Herod; he offered to let Jesus go as part of a holiday tradition; and he washed his hands of the matter. Being popular, though, meant sending an innocent man to his death – and in the heat of the moment, Pilate was willing to pay the price.

The story doesn't end there, though. Pilate ultimately did what was right instead of what was popular; he told the world who Jesus was, and he didn't back down.

In terms of religion, we have to make a decision much like Pilate made – we have to decide what we are going to do with Jesus. We need to look at the evidence and decide if he is a myth, a good teacher, or the Messiah. We are going to be asked to publicly proclaim what we decide.

This story teaches more than religion, though. It teaches about leadership. It reminds us that if we are going to be a good leader and do the right thing, we may not be popular. Will you stand up for what is right, even when those around you won't?

QUESTIONS TO PONDER

- If I were Pilate and had to face the angry mob, what would I have done? Why?

- If I become a Christian, I will likely be asked to profess Jesus as my Lord and Savior in front of a church congregation. Does that scare me? Why or why not?

- When was the last time I had to tell my friends no to doing something they wanted me to do? How do I deal with negative peer pressure?

PRAYER

"Almighty Father, help me to be as innocent and courageous as Jesus, staying silent and strong when I am tried. May I rebuke the evil in my mind and stand with dignity and integrity, just as Jesus did, even when His life was in others' hands. Amen."

CHAPTER 44

JESUS IS NAILED TO THE CROSS: LOVE YOUR ENEMIES

*Do not gloat when your enemy falls;
when they stumble, do not let your heart rejoice,*

- Proverbs 24:17

THE STORY

As Jesus carried his cross to The Skull to be crucified, he stumbled, for he was weak from the 39 lashes he had received. Some of the soldiers escorting him grabbed a man out of the crowd, Simon of Cyrene, and made him carry the cross the rest of the way behind Jesus.

A large crowd was following Jesus; some were crying for him, and some were crying, "Crucify him!" Jesus, though, was not the only one proceeding to The Skull that day. Two criminals were also proceeding. When the procession got to The Skull, the soldiers nailed the three men to crosses, placing Jesus in the middle. As they nailed Him to the cross, Jesus said, "Father, forgive them. They don't know what they are doing."

The crowd watched as He hung, dying. Jesus saw his mother and His disciple John, and He asked John to look after her. Soldiers gambled for His clothes. Guards brought a sign that read "This is the King of the Jews" from Pilate to hang on the cross. A soldier mocked Him by offering bitter wine. Many in the crowd mocked Jesus, saying, "If you are the king of the Jews, save yourself." Even one of the criminals said, "If you're the Messiah, save yourself and save us!"

Hearing this, the other criminal rebuked the first, saying, "Don't you respect God? We're getting what we deserved, but he didn't do anything wrong." He turned to Jesus and said, "Remember me when you come into power."

Jesus replied, "Today, you will be with me in paradise."

Because the next day was the Sabbath and the Jews did not want any bodies up at that time, the Jews asked Pilate to break the legs of the three men so they would die quicker. Pilate gave permission, and soldiers broke the legs of the two criminals, but when they came to Jesus, they noted He was already dead. To ensure He was dead, a soldier pierced His side with a spear, allowing blood and water to gush from Him. Jesus was dead – there was no doubt.

DEVOTIONAL THOUGHT

Have you ever been mistreated? Have you ever been accused of doing something that you did not do? Have you ever been teased by people whom you thought were your friends? On Sunday, Jesus had ridden into town on a donkey, just as King Solomon had when he was made king, and not even a week later, some of those same people were in another mob yelling, "Crucify him."

It would have been easy to wish vengeance upon the soldier who drove the spikes into his hands and feet. It would have been tempting to spit on the soldier who offered him a bitter drink when he thirsted for something refreshing. It would have been easy to snap back at the rude criminal hanging beside him. Through all of this, though, Jesus prayed, "Father, forgive them."

Jesus talked about turning the other cheek in His sermons; on the cross, He demonstrated how to react to those who hurt you. By following Jesus's example, we become the bigger person, and should they continue to insult or hurt us, we make them look bad in front of others. Returning insult for insult, one would likely escalate the situation; by praying for our enemies, we defuse the crisis. By forgiving our enemies, we free ourselves from having to carry a grudge; even though he was in physical pain, Jesus was at peace.

- *When someone teases me, taunts me, or hits me, what can I do instead of doing the same thing back at them?*

- *Why should I forgive my enemies?*

- *Is "forgiving" the same thing as "forgive and forget"? Why or why not?*

PRAYER

"Almighty Father, I ask for the strength to forgive those who have wronged me, even if I never receive an apology. Help me to release any bitterness and pray for those who have hurt me. I know true peace comes from a forgiving heart, as You desire. Amen."

CHAPTER 45

THE RESURRECTION OF JESUS: WHY IT MATTERS

> *25 Jesus said to her, "I am the resurrection and the life. The one who believes in me will live, even though they die; 26 and whoever lives by believing in me will never die. Do you believe this?"*
>
> *- John 11:25-26*

THE STORY

Jesus was dead. He died nailed to a cross. To make sure that he was dead, a guard had jabbed a spear into his side. In the late afternoon of the day Jesus died, Joseph, a follower of Jesus, went to the Roman governor, Pilate, and asked for Jesus's body. Pilate issued an order that the body be given to Joseph. Joseph wrapped the body in a long sheet of linen and then placed it in a tomb he had made for himself carved out of rock. Disciples and others watched as Joseph rolled a huge boulder in front of the tomb, a rock that was practically immovable.

The religious leaders then went to Pilate and stated, "While he was alive, that liar Jesus said that he would rise again after three days. Therefore, we ask that you make the tomb secure for three days so no one can steal the body and create a hoax."

"Take some of my soldiers," Pilate invited. "Make the tomb as secure as you can." The priests stationed the guards outside the tomb; they also sealed the tomb and affixed a stamp that would have to be broken if the tomb was to be entered.

All was calm until very early Sunday morning. At that time, an angel rolled aside the stone and sat on it. The angel had a face that looked like lightning and snow-white clothes. The guards, grizzly men who had seen the horrors of war, fainted in fear.

About this time, as dawn was breaking, women arrived with spices, hoping to be allowed to anoint Jesus's body. The angel called to them, "Why do you look for the living among the dead? He is not here; he has risen!"

The women rushed to the Upper Room to tell the disciples and other believers about seeing the empty tomb and about what they had heard. What they said sounded like nonsense. Still, upon hearing the news, Peter and John raced to the tomb to see for themselves.

John got to the tomb first, bent over, and saw strips of linen lying on the ground. Peter wasn't so cautious; he ran straight inside the tomb. Inside, he saw more strips of linen as well as the cloth that had been wrapped around Jesus's head. John then went inside and looked around with Peter; neither remembered that Jesus had said He would rise from the dead. After they were done investigating, they went back to tell the others what they had seen.

DEVOTIONAL THOUGHT

The Resurrection of Jesus is what sets Jesus apart from anyone else. If He had not risen, the Christmas story would have been just another extraordinary birth. If He had not risen, He would have been just another good teacher. The fact that He arose from the dead shows that He conquered death, assured His disciples that he had secured their salvation, and motivated His followers to speak boldly. The Resurrection also reminds us that God has reign over both life and death, and if God says that something lives, it lives.

The Resurrection was a historical event with hundreds of witnesses. As time progressed, history became legend, legend became lore, and lore became myth. Many people have heard the myth so much that it has lost its original punch; they have realized the myth-like storytelling and have forgotten it was based on facts. Perhaps it's a biased statement, but the Resurrection is the greatest event in human history.

When the Resurrection happened, the disciples did not know what to make of it; they did not understand that Jesus had to rise from the dead – and these were Jesus's closest followers. If the resurrection and Christianity seem confusing, you aren't alone. Through study, prayer, and hanging around other believers, the meaning of it will get clearer and clearer. "He is risen" is more than a greeting; it is a statement of fact.

QUESTIONS TO PONDER

- *Do I believe the resurrection is real? Why or why not?*
- *What difference does it matter if the resurrection is real?*

PRAYER

"Almighty Father, I believe in the resurrection, even though it happened long ago when there were no cameras to capture it. I trust that You designed it this way so that we may live in faith, believing without seeing. Strengthen my faith in Your truth. Amen."

CHAPTER 46

DOUBTING THOMAS: IT'S OKAY TO ASK QUESTIONS

> *Be merciful to those who doubt;*
>
> *- Jude 22*

THE STORY

On Easter morning, the disciples had learned that the stone that sealed Jesus's grave had been rolled away and the body was missing. Throughout the day, various people around Jerusalem reported seeing Jesus. The disciples as a group, though, had not seen Jesus.

The disciples feared being arrested by the Jewish leaders, but they decided to get together that evening in the Upper Room to discuss the day. Once every one of the Twelve was assembled except Judas, who had betrayed Jesus, and Thomas, who was running late, was present, they locked the doors and began to discuss the day's events. As they were reflecting, Jesus came and stood among them, saying, "Peace be with you." He showed them his nail-scarred hands and his side, which had been pierced with a spear. The disciples were overjoyed. Jesus shared a few thoughts with them and then disappeared.

When Thomas finally arrived, the other disciples told him enthusiastically, "We have seen the Lord."

Thomas wanted to believe them, but he had his doubts. "Unless I see the nail marks on his hands, put my fingers where the nails were, and put my hand into his side, I will not believe."

A week later, the Twelve, aside from Judas, were in the meeting place again. Like the week before, the doors were locked, but Jesus came and stood among them. "Peace be with you," he greeted. He then turned to Thomas and said, "See these holes in my hand; put your fingers in them. Reach out your hand here and feel my side. Stop doubting; believe."

"My Lord and my God!" Thomas said in reverence.

"You believe because you have seen me; blessed are those who have not seen but still believe."

DEVOTIONAL THOUGHT

How do scientists learn new knowledge? They ask questions, technically known as research questions. By asking questions, they can begin to search for answers.

It is okay to have questions about God. By asking questions and seeking answers, you will come to a better understanding of God and grow closer to Him. It is also okay to have doubts; like Thomas, people who love God have doubts about things. Religious scholars, monks, and seminary professors devote their lives to studying religion, but they will be the first to admit that they don't know all the answers.

Asking questions is how we learn, not just about religion but about life in general. By asking questions, we begin the quest of finding knowledge. For instance, if you want to learn about beetles, you have to ask questions such as "How did they get the name beetle?" and "Where do beetles live?" Likewise, the human mind may not be able to comprehend God, but by asking specific questions, we can at least learn a little about Him.

QUESTIONS TO PONDER

- What else besides what's in this book would I like to know about the Bible?

- What does "seeing is believing" mean? What did Jesus mean when He said, "Blessed are those who have not seen but still believe?"

- What was life like in the Upper Room during those seven days when Thomas and the other disciples shared very different opinions about Jesus? (You notice they were still friends when Jesus appeared the second time.) What can I do to better get along with people who don't believe quite the way I do?

PRAYER

"Almighty Father, I confess that my heart often struggles with doubt, unable to grasp the depth of faith needed to trust fully in You. Please help my unbelief and guide my heart to the right place, where faith overcomes doubt and I trust in You completely. Amen."

CHAPTER 47

JESUS AND THE MIRACULOUS CATCH: NOW WHAT?

 *4 When he had finished speaking, he said to Simon, "Put out into deep water, and let down the nets for a catch."*
5 Simon answered, "Master, we've worked hard all night and haven't caught anything. But because you say so, I will let down the nets."

- Luke 5:4-5

The disciples had seen the resurrected Jesus twice – once in the Upper Room without Thomas and a week later in the Upper Room with Thomas - and they now believed that He had risen from the dead. The shock of the past few days had kept them together in the Upper Room, where they kept a low profile to avoid being arrested. The realization that they had to move on with their lives was beginning to dawn on them. Funds were running low, so one evening, Peter announced, "I'm going fishing."

Prior to becoming an assistant to Jesus, several of the Twelve had been career fishermen. His fishing partners, James and John, said, "We'll come too," and four other disciples joined in as well.

They fished all night, but they caught nothing. As the morning dawned, a man on the beach called, "Have you caught any fish?"

"No," they confessed.

"Throw your net on the right-hand side of the boat, and you'll get some," he said.

They did as he suggested, and they couldn't haul the net in because it held so many fish.

As they struggled with the net, John suddenly placed the voice and proclaimed, "It's the Lord."

When Peter heard this, he put on his tunic – he had stripped to his underwear for work – jumped into the water and headed toward shore. The other disciples stayed with the boat, towing the fish to shore. When they got to the shore, they found breakfast waiting -fish cooking over a fire and bread. "Bring some of the fish you caught," Jesus said, and Peter went out to the boat and helped drag the net ashore.

"Have some breakfast," Jesus invited. (No one dared to ask, "Who are you?" for they knew it was the Lord.) He then served the bread and the fish.

After breakfast, Jesus asked Peter in front of everyone, "Peter, do you love me?"

"Yes, Lord, you know I love you."

"Then feed my lambs," Jesus said, and Peter understood what he meant. Jesus was the Good Shepherd, and Peter was meant to tend his sheep, to preach and teach people about God and the Resurrected Jesus, not to go back to his prior career of fishing.

DEVOTIONAL THOUGHT

Have you ever accomplished a goal? Did you learn to ride a bike? Did you pass to the next grade level at school? When you first accomplished the goal, you likely felt feelings of elation, but after the celebration ended, your life likely felt empty. You then began to look for new challenges.

Peter and the other disciples experienced great elation; they knew that Jesus had risen from the dead. They were so happy about this the first two weeks. However, the questions of "So what?" and "Now what?" occupied their minds. They knew Jesus was resurrected, but they weren't sure how to respond or what to do with this knowledge.

All of us face "So what?" and "Now what?" moments. Having read this book, you will have to answer those questions to give your life direction. When you graduate from school, you will encounter those questions again. When there is a major event in your life, such as a parent getting transferred to another town, you've got to face those questions. Going back to the way things used to be, just like Peter tried, is always an option, but in many cases, new adventures await.

QUESTIONS TO PONDER

- *What are two of my current goals? What opportunities does meeting these goals offer me?*

- *Where do I see myself ten years from now? Twenty-five years from now?*

- *If the resurrection of Jesus is true, does it affect my life in any way?*

PRAYER

"Almighty Father, I know that without Your guidance, I can accomplish nothing. Just as You filled the disciples' nets with fish, make my efforts fruitful as I share the Gospel with others. Help me to rely on Your strength and wisdom in all I do. Amen."

CHAPTER 48

>>>>>>>>>>>>>>>>>>>>>>>>>>>✝<<<<<<<<<<<<<<<<<<<<<<<<<

THE DAY OF PENTECOST - THE BIRTHDAY OF THE CHURCH: BACKING UP WHAT YOU BELIEVE

> "
> *And these signs will accompany those who believe: In my name they will drive out demons; they will speak in new tongues;*
>
> *- Mark 16:17*
> "

THE STORY

On the Day of Pentecost, the Twelve and their friends met together again in the Upper Room. Pentecost was a feast to celebrate the wheat harvest; it was also to celebrate the giving of the Ten Commandments. Pentecost was commanded in the book of Exodus, and any Jew who could traveled to Jerusalem to celebrate it.

It had been 50 days since Jesus's death and resurrection. The Twelve and their friends were reminiscing in the Upper Room when the sound of a windstorm filled their room, and what looked like tongues of fire appeared above their heads. Each person present was filled with the Holy Spirit and began speaking languages they didn't know.

Many people heard the roaring sound in the sky and rushed to see what it was about. When they got to the house, they were shocked to hear the disciples talking flawlessly in their native language about the mighty miracles of God. "What is going on?" they pondered, listening to the disciples. "These are simple men from Galilee, and yet they speak about God in our language."

"They're drunk!" someone called.

The eleven apostles turned to face the mob that had gathered. Peter stated, "These men aren't drunk. It is barely 9 a.m.; people don't get drunk at 9 a.m. What you are seeing was predicted years ago by the prophets." Peter then preached a long sermon, explaining everything, talking about Jesus, and urging people to commit their lives to Jesus.

About three thousand people were baptized that day. These three thousand people joined other believers in the apostles' teaching sessions, Communion services, and prayer meetings. They, in turn, ministered to other people, and what later became known as Christianity – the term means "little Christ" - began to be spread across the world.

DEVOTIONAL THOUGHT

Do you have opinions that you want to persuade others about? Peter did. He was of the opinion that the disciples were under the influence of the Holy Spirit. He didn't call those who didn't agree with him poo-poo heads or suggest that they be put in prison; he simply tried to convince them that he was right. He did this by providing reasons for his belief; he did this by pointing out that their explanation made no sense because no one got drunk at 9 a.m. and then explained why his explanation made sense.

When you have to argue a point, you may be tempted to call people on the other side names, but name-calling doesn't help people understand your view. You must share reasons for why you feel the way you do.

Once you have shared why you feel as you do, be sure to answer the question, "So what?" Once Peter had convinced his listeners that the Holy Spirit was upon them and that Jesus had risen from the dead, Peter answered the question of "so what" by having people get baptized and become a part of the Church. When we make a case and have convinced someone we are right, we must let them know what to do now that they have been persuaded to see things our way.

QUESTIONS TO PONDER

- *Some people made fun of the disciples' babbling in incoherent languages. When someone makes fun of my accent, what do I do? What should I do?*

- *If I had to make a case for something – the case might be as complex as "you need Jesus as your savior" to as personal as "I want to stay up late tonight," how would I convince others to see my point of view?*

- *Peter, the man who denied knowing Jesus three times on the night Jesus was arrested, now boldly stood in front of people proclaiming Jesus as his Lord. Why was he weak one day and 54 days later incredibly bold?*

PRAYER

"Almighty Father, I desire to be like Peter, the rock upon which Your church was built. Help me speak to people from different cultures, sharing Your Gospel across borders, both in person and online. Strengthen my faith with reason, so I may boldly spread Your truth. Amen."

CHAPTER 49

PAUL AND SILAS IN PRISON: PRAISE GOD IN ALL CIRCUMSTANCES

 *16 Rejoice always, 17 pray continually, 18 give thanks in all circumstances; for this is God's will for you in Christ Jesus.*

- 1 Thessalonians 5:16-18

In the years following Jesus's death, people began to preach and teach about him. While the message was accepted as gospel by some people, many people were disgusted with what they were hearing. Preachers like Paul and Silas often went to the town square and began to preach, and sometimes, the town officials would arrest them for disturbing the peace.

One night around midnight, Paul and Silas were in jail for disturbing the peace; their backs hurt from the floggings they had received, and their feet were in stocks, but they were praying and singing hymns to God. Paul and Silas were in the center cage, and, like spokes on a wheel, the other prisoners were around them. The jailor was outside their cell and had been commanded to guard them carefully. Ironically, he had fallen asleep listening to them, but the prisoners around them listened.

Suddenly, an earthquake shook the prison walls, the prison doors flew open, and everyone's chains came loose. The jailer woke up with a jerk, and when he saw the prison doors open, he thought all the prisoners had escaped. He knew he would be held responsible, so he drew his sword to kill himself.

Standing in his cell, Paul watched the jailor draw his sword and knew why he was doing it; he shouted, "Don't harm yourself! We are all here!"

"We are all here? Is that really what he heard? The jailer called for lights. He ran frantically from cell to cell, verifying the inmates were still there, even though the cell doors were wide open and the prisoner's shackles were removed. Having made a full circle, he rushed into Paul and Silas' cell and fell trembling before them.

He then composed himself, rose, and asked that they accompany him to his desk. His family was already at his desk; they had come from their nearby quarters to ensure the jailer and the prisoners were okay following the earthquake. With the eyes of all the prisoners and his family on him, the jailor turned to Paul and Silas and asked, "Sirs, what must I do to be a follower of Jesus?"

Paul and Silas replied, "Believe in the Lord Jesus, and you will be saved—you and your household," and then they proceeded to tell the jailer and his family all the stories of Jesus, including the Resurrection. Having heard what Paul and Silas had to say, the jailor and his whole family began believing in God!

Paul and Silas had been beaten by the city officials before being tossed into jail. The jailer noticed the wounds and washed them; Paul and Silas then used the water to baptize the jailer and his household. The jailer's family then took Paul and Silas to their quarters and fixed a meal for them.

When it was daylight, the city officials sent an officer to the jail. The officer whispered to the jailer, who then smiled and told Paul, "The city officials have ordered that you and Silas are to be released. You can leave now. Go in peace."

The jailer was happy for Paul and Silas. To his surprise, though, Paul replied, "I'm not going anywhere yet. They beat us publicly without a trial, even though we are Roman citizens, and they threw us into prison. And now they want to get rid of us quietly? No way! Tell them to come here and escort us out."

The jailer and the officer looked at each other in confusion. Finally, the jailer said, "You heard the man. Go tell the magistrates."

The officer did as he was requested. When he told the magistrates that Paul and Silas were Roman citizens – they did not realize that the two Jews had dual citizenship. They knew they had made a terrible mistake. If Paul reported what they had done to their superiors, they would likely lose their jobs. Wanting to make amends, they went to the jail and personally escorted Paul and Silas from the prison.

DEVOTIONAL THOUGHT

Have you ever had a bad day, a day in which nothing seems to go right? Paul and Silas were having a bad day. They had been beaten and thrown into prison; their rights as Roman citizens had been totally disregarded. They were hurting; they were confused – they had been trying to do God's work, but God didn't stop the mob from attacking them. In such a situation, when things are going poorly, and one feels abandoned by even God, it is tempting to curse God, go into a deep depression, or engage in dangerous behavior. What did Paul and Silas do, though? They praised God.

God didn't promise that being a Christian would be easy. In fact, being a believer often results in a much harder life than not being one. What He did promise, though, is that He will not forsake us. We can have inner peace in the worst of situations. Paul and Silas were able to praise God on one of the worst days of their lives.

QUESTIONS TO PONDER

- *Why does God allow His people to suffer?*

- *When I am going through tough times, what can I do to remind myself that God has not forsaken me?*

- *Paul didn't expect to be arrested; he was a citizen, but he was arrested anyway. In life, we often don't expect what happens next. When an unexpected change takes place, what can I do to adjust?*

PRAYER

"Almighty Father, help me praise You not only in the good times but also in the difficult moments. Under all circumstances, I want to draw near to You, soaking in Your goodness and seeing the silver lining. Even when it's hard, I choose to trust in Your goodness. Amen."

CHAPTER 50

THE NEW WORLD: TIMES ARE BAD, THEY'RE GOING TO GET WORSE, BUT GOOD WILL TRIUMPH

> *"As the new heavens and the new earth that I make will endure before me," declares the Lord, "so will your name and descendants endure.*
>
> *- Isaiah 66:22*

THE STORY

John, a pastor who had been exiled for preaching the gospel, was pondering whether God could ever overcome the evil that he saw in the world; he wanted to believe that God was superior, but his being exiled and the struggles of God's people caused him to wonder. God saw his plight and sent an angel to him.

John didn't recognize the angel at first; he looked just like a typical man carrying a scroll. However, as the angel spoke about the future and showed John what was to come – that God would one day restore Eden and that death would be no more – John realized that he was speaking to an angel. As soon as he realized this, he fell down to worship at the angel's feet.

"Don't do that," the angel demanded. "I am a servant of the Lord, just like you are and all who keep the words I have shared with you. Worship God."

"But . . ."

"The Lord sent me, his servant, to you to show you the things that must take place. He is the Alpha and the Omega, the First and the Last, the Beginning and the End. He and He alone is worthy of your worship – and He is coming back soon."

John had heard from the angel all the terrible things that God was going to permit to take place before He returned, terrible things that He hoped would encourage people to rely on Him. John so looked forward to the return of Jesus that he was now willing to endure those things, and said, "Come, Lord Jesus, come."

DEVOTIONAL THOUGHT

Have you ever heard someone say, "God is dead?" These people believe that if there was a God, He was not eternal, for He would never have let the world become as vile as it has become. John, one of the Twelve, had watched Jesus ascend into Heaven and had heard Him say that He would be back shortly, but "shortly" had turned into several decades; people were beginning to doubt if He was coming back. If you've ever wondered if God exists, you're not the first to ask.

John could see the world getting more and more vile around him. Why would a loving God let so much bad go on in the world? To his shock, John learned that it was going to get a lot worse before He puts a halt to it. However, he did learn God's reasoning. One, it gives people like yourself a chance to be born and to participate in it. Two, it gives people who haven't turned to God yet a chance to turn to him.

Are Christians perfect? No. John had a strong faith, but even he was questioning God's strength, God's wisdom, and if he had heard Jesus correctly. Also, John was rebuked because he started to worship an angel. John loved the Lord and had spent his life preaching and teaching, but he was still growing in his faith. We, too, must wrestle with our faith. Christians don't know everything about God – that's why it's called faith, but they do know that God is good and, therefore, can say with confidence, "Come, Lord Jesus, come."

QUESTIONS TO PONDER

- *In my opinion, why hasn't the Second Coming happened?*

- *By sharing the way the world will transform from the corrupt state it is in today into an eternal paradise John is trying to provide comfort. He shared that the tough times aren't going to last. Do I share his optimism? Why or why not?*

- *What are some questions I have about the Bible?*

- *Do I see examples of God being active in my life? If so, what are they?*

PRAYER

"Almighty Father, I trust that You will triumph in the end, even as we face difficult times. Though I may not understand Your reasons, I believe they are beyond my comprehension. Help me hold fast to my faith, knowing that the glory of the new heaven and earth will make it all worth it. Amen."

www.ingramcontent.com/pod-product-compliance
Lightning Source LLC
Chambersburg PA
CBHW060817120626
46557CB00001B/249